THE Healthy Life Cookbook

CONTENTS

Introduction 7

Low Fat 13

Dairy Free 61

Low Sugar Treats 109

Paleo 157

Vegetarian 205

Comfort Food 253

Index 302

INTRODUCTION

A healthy diet used to be seen as something a little bit extreme, generally involving tofu — but that's not the case anymore. These days the quest for healthy eating is on everybody's agenda, and the principles are generally understood: eating fresh food is good, processed food not so good; some fats are good and others not so; and maybe a whole heap of white sugar might send the body into a rush and then a slump. If you want to delve further that's possible too, and, as ever, some people go to extremes and embrace a fully vegan, sugar-free or 'Paleo' diet, for example. In this book we introduce you to all of these ideas, and provide an overview of the best kinds of food to eat for each, along with plenty of straightforward and tasty recipes to make it easy. If you try a little bit of everything in this book, and don't deprive yourself of occasional treats, you'll be well on the way to living a healthy life.

All fats were not created equal. We know that now. In the first chapter of this book we celebrate the good fats — that's unsaturated fats, which are found in plentiful supply in avocados, fish, nuts, eggs, seeds and some grains. These foods boast high levels of omega-3 fatty acids that are thought to help reduce cholesterol levels and reduce inflammation, among other health benefits. We celebrate these foods with lots of great recipes ideas for how to incorporate more of them into your day-to-day cooking. Saturated fats fall into two camps: the trans fats, which are best avoided, and the others, which are found in red meat and dairy and are best eaten in moderation.

Some people find dairy hard to tolerate, and the number of people this affects is on the rise. Others prefer to limit dairy as they try to reduce their consumption of saturated fat. If giving up or reducing dairy intake feels scary, then help is at hand in the next section of this book. First up, we introduce you to the easier-than-you-could-imagine recipe for making your own nut milk. Add a bit of cocoa and that's a glass of chocolate milk every bit as delicious as the pre-made versions in supermarkets. Coconut milk also features in this section as the perfect ingredient for making dairy-free and delicious yoghurts, ice creams and other desserts. If you are worried that dairy-free means low calcium levels, don't be. You just need to eat your greens, and we offer lots of fun new ways to do so in the recipes in this section.

Low sugar has to be the buzz phrase of the moment, and whatever you think of the attention it's currently getting, you can't deny that we eat a lot of it and it sneaks into the most likely and unlikely of packaged food. One simple way to reduce your sugar intake is to not buy packaged food. But there are lots of other positive steps you can take to gradually or even just occasionally replace processed white sugar with sugars that will be kinder to your body, such as coconut sugar, raw honey, maple syrup or sweeteners like stevia and natvia. We give the low-down on sugar replacements in this section, and offer a whole host of delicious recipes for familiar food such as ice cream and sorbet, muffins, cookies and tarts, as well as food that's a bit different, such as raw cheesecakes and bliss balls. Best of all in this section, we celebrate ingredients that are naturally sweet, even if you might not think it, such as pumpkin, sweet potato and onions. You'll find recipes here for pumpkin scones, cookies and bread, and sweet onion tarts.

Next on the list of current healthy eating trends has to be the 'Paleo diet'. That's a reference to Paleolithic, when about 2.5 million years ago cavemen ate whatever they could get their hands on — usually meat, fish and whatever was in season or

Healthy

[ac·tive] adjective

enjoying health and vigour of body,
mind, or spirit

— MERRIAM-WEBSTER

could be easily preserved. It's not a bad set of principles to adhere too, although some critics feel too many food groups are excluded from the Paleo diet. Like all things, it is good in moderation and can be fun to explore. In this section of the book we provide some simple and tasty Paleo-friendly meals, with a focus on fish, meat and offal. Offal has been making a comeback with chefs recently, and it's surprisingly easy and affordable to cook with. In this section you'll find recipes for cooking with liver, including a simple chicken liver pate recipe that will make you wonder why you ever bought the stuff. Fermentation is another big focus of this section of the book. If you've ever wanted to know how to make your own pickles, sauerkraut or kombucha, you'll find out here.

Many health-oriented foodies swear by a vegetarian diet, claiming that meat is too much for our digestive systems. Or maybe it's simply that too much meat is too much. Anyway, vegetarian food has made a comeback. Step aside, tofu burgers. Enter, zoodles (that's pasta made from vegetables like zucchini) and cauliflower steaks, cauliflower rice and cauliflower tacos. In this section we celebrate the mighty purple eggplant, with recipes for eggplant pate, eggplant chips and hearty stuffed eggplant. If ever vegetables were to step up to the plate as meat replacements, cauliflower and eggplant are surely the ones for the task.

Last but not least, we celebrate comfort food. There's an assumption that healthy eating means no treats and no indulgence. Not so. An increased awareness about food allows us to substitute the old-school gluten or sugar-filled recipes with ingredients such as quinoa or vegetables and sweeteners used in new and creative ways. So here you'll find healthy versions of all the classics, such as burgers, pizza, pasta, roast dinners, chocolate cake and ice cream.

Enjoy *The Healthy Life!*

Low Fat

THE SKINNY ON FATS

Fat is often thought of as a dirty word. It's not. Bodies and brains need 'good' fat everyday — and not all 'bad' fat is all bad either.

GOOD FATS

Unsaturated fats are the healthiest, and they help satisfy hunger so there are fewer cravings for sweet and naughty things. The monounsaturated and polyunsaturated varieties are found in avocados, fish, nuts, eggs and some grains. These fats have some magical medical benefits. Monounsaturated fats help inflammation and are good for the heart. Polyunsaturated fats, also known as omega-3s, are essential for the function of brain, heart and blood. All good fats help reduce cholesterol and play a role in balancing out blood sugar and insulin for people with diabetes and for those with a sweet tooth.

BAD FATS

There are two types of 'bad' fats: trans fats raise cholesterol and do no good. Luckily, many food brands and even fast-food chains regulate use of trans fats. In general, look for anything that says 'partially hydrogenated oils', and avoid those foods.

Saturated fats are a little more complex — over the years, research has shown that they can have a balancing effect on cholesterol levels. While they can raise bad cholesterol, they can also raise good cholesterol. The best approach is eat in moderation and eat more unsaturated fats. Saturated fats are found in red meat and dairy. Be aware of fat content in foods and plan meals around the good ones.

DELICIOUS 'GOOD FAT' FOODS!

AVOCADOS: This wonder fruit tastes luxurious because it is full of good fat. Use on toast instead of butter, on potatoes instead of sour cream, and feel no guilt about guacamole at party time.

PARMESAN CHEESE: Yes! It is relatively high in fat, and about half is healthy fats. Parmesan also has more protein and calcium than any other cheese, so it's a good choice for cheese lovers to satisfy their cravings.

WALNUTS, PISTACHIOS, ALMONDS: Walnuts are the super-nut. A handful will give a day's blast of omega-3 fats. Pecans, pistachios, and almonds also contain vitamin E as well as minerals for eye heath.

OLIVES: One cup of black olives has 15 grams of fat, most of it good monounsaturated fat. A bowl of olives for a snack is never a bad idea, though take note of the sodium content, which is higher in some brands than others.

Teriyaki Salmon Bowl

FRESH CONTEMPORARY STYLE AND FLAVOURS ABOUND IN THIS
GREAT MIDWEEK DINNER THAT'S READY IN 30 MINUTES

SERVES 2

SAUCE

2 tbsps tamari (or soy sauce)

¼ cup (60ml, 2fl oz) mirin (or dry sherry)

½ tbsp fresh ginger, minced

1 clove garlic, minced

1½ tsps honey

1 tsp sesame oil

½ tbsp water

1 tsp cornflour

SALMON BOWL

2 x 150g (5oz) salmon fillets

100g (3½ oz) snow peas, ends trimmed

1 small carrot, grated

1 cup (100g, 4oz) bean sprouts

½ Lebanese cucumber, seeds removed, halved and sliced

Handful of watercress

1 radish, sliced

1 cup (160g, 6oz) cooked rice

1 tsp toasted sesame seeds, white or black

2 spring onions, sliced

Preheat the oven to 200°C (400°F, Gas Mark 6). Line a small baking tray with baking paper.

In a small saucepan over medium heat mix together the tamari, mirin, ginger, garlic, honey and sesame oil.

Mix the cornflour and water together in a small bowl. Pour the cornflour mixture into the saucepan and stir vigorously as the mixture will immediately start to thicken. Reduce the heat to low and keep stirring for 2 minutes until it becomes the consistency of a thick sauce. Reserve 1 teaspoon of the sauce.

Brush the salmon fillets with the sauce and then place them skin side down on the baking tray. Bake in the oven for 15 minutes until the salmon is mostly cooked.

Remove from the oven and allow it to rest for 5 minutes. Dispose of the skin.

Bring a small saucepan of lightly salted water to the boil. Add snow peas, carrot and bean sprouts and boil for 1 minute. Drain and rinse immediately in cold water.

In a small bowl, mix the bean sprouts with 1 teaspoon of sauce and 1 teaspooon of water.

Serve the salmon on rice with vegetables, sesame seeds and spring onion sprinkled over as a garnish.

Red Curry Salmon with Sauteed Greens

AN EASY, LIGHT AND SWEETLY SAUCY DINNER OPTION THAT'S
FULL OF FLAVOUR

SERVES 4

600g (1lb 5oz) salmon
fillet

2 tsps coconut oil

2 tbsps red curry paste

1 tsp honey

1 tsp fish sauce

1/3 cup (100ml, 3½ fl oz)
coconut milk

¾ cup (200ml, 7fl oz)
vegetable stock

1 tbsp fresh lime juice

4 bunches baby bok
choy, ends trimmed

2 bunches Chinese
broccoli

Heat the coconut oil in a large frying pan over medium heat.

Fry the curry paste for 1 minute, stirring continuously.

Mix in the honey and fish sauce, then gradually add the coconut
milk, stirring while you pour it in. Then stir through the stock.

Place the salmon in the pan, skin side down, and cook for
5 minutes. Spoon the sauce over the fillet while it cooks. Gently
flip the fillet over and cook for a further 4 minutes or until the
fillet is cooked through. Remove the fillet from the pan, cover
with foil and set aside.

Bring the sauce to the boil, reduce the heat and let it simmer for
5 minutes until it has reduced to a thick sauce.

Steam the bok choy and broccoli for 5 minutes until softened.

Serve the salmon with the bok choy and broccoli, with the sauce
poured over.

Hipster Salad with Avocado Vinaigrette

ENERGY - BOOSTING GRAINS MEET GOOD FATS AND GOOD
TIMES IN THIS WHOLESOME, HEALTHY SALAD

SERVES 4

4 cups (550g, 1¼ lb) butternut pumpkin, cut into 2cm (1in) cubes

2 tbsps olive oil

Salt and freshly ground pepper

2 cups (340g, 12oz) uncooked quinoa

2 bunches broccolini, ends trimmed

2 spring onions, sliced

200g (7oz) rocket

1 cup (50g, 2oz) micro greens (cress)

½ cup (60g, 2oz) pistachios, roughly chopped

1 large pomegranate, seeded

3 large avocados, halved and sliced — reserve ¼ cup (45g, 1½ oz) avocado for the dressing

DRESSING

1 clove garlic, minced

¼ cup (60ml, 2fl oz) olive oil

2 tbsps apple cider vinegar

2 tbsps lemon juice

Preheat oven to 220°C (425°F, Gas Mark 7). Line a large flat baking tray with baking paper.

Toss the cubed pumpkin with half the olive oil and a couple of good grinds of salt and pepper.

Place the pumpkin on the baking tray and bake for 40 minutes or until the cubes are slightly browned on the outside and cooked through. Remove from the oven and place in a large bowl.

To cook the quinoa, add it to 4 cups (1L, 2pt) of salted water in a large saucepan and bring to the boil. Reduce the heat, cover and let it simmer for 20 minutes, or until quinoa is cooked.

Bring a second large saucepan of salted water to the boil. Cook the broccolini for 2 minutes, then remove and rinse immediately in cold water. Add to the bowl with the pumpkin.

Once the quinoa is ready, place it in the bowl with the vegetables, along with the spring onions, rocket, greens, pistachios and pomegranate seeds and toss everything to combine.

To make the dressing, blend together or use a stick blender to puree the garlic, olive oil, vinegar, lemon juice, a grind of salt and pepper and the reserved avocado. Puree until smooth, adding more lemon juice as needed to thin it out.

To serve, place slices of avocado on top of the salad mix and drizzle over the dressing.

BAKED AVO EGGS

High five to avocado for its awesome health benefits. All of us, but especially pregnant women, should embrace the avo for the good fats, dietary fibre and folate it contains. Is this goodness diminished by cooking? Good question. It seems little research has been done on this but it is known that the fat in avocado is mainly monounsaturated, a more heat stable fat. So the odds are in favour of avocado retaining it's goodness when baked. Either way, raw or baked, it's delicious.

Kale Salad

SERVES 4–6

2 bunches kale

2 pears, cubed

3 tbsps olive oil

¼ tsp salt

¼ tsp pepper

2 avocados, halved and sliced

¼ cup (5g, ¼ oz) fresh basil leaves

3 tbsps pine nuts

1 lemon, cut into wedges

1 tsp paprika

Wash kale and cut out the stems. Slice into 3cm-wide (1in) pieces. Place into a large mixing bowl with the pear.

Toss the pear and kale thoroughly with 2 tablespoons of the olive oil, plus salt and pepper.

To serve, place the avocado and pine nuts on top of the kale and pear.

Drizzle over remaining olive oil, a few leaves of basil, a squeeze of lemon juice and a dusting of paprika.

Avocado Fries with Yoghurt Dip

SERVES 2

½ lemon, cut into wedges

2 large avocados, halved and cut into thick slices

¼ cup (30g, 1oz) plain flour

Pinch of paprika

Salt and pepper

2 eggs, beaten

1¼ cups (155g, 5oz) breadcrumbs

¼ cup (60ml, 2fl oz) olive oil

YOGHURT DIP

2 tsps olive oil

½ cup (125g, 4oz) Greek yoghurt

1 clove garlic, crushed

1 tbsp flat-leaf parsley, finely chopped

Preheat oven to 200°C (400°F, Gas Mark 6). Line a baking tray with baking paper. To make the dip, mix ingredients and set aside. Squeeze lemon juice over avocado slices. Mix paprika, flour and a pinch of salt and pepper. Coat slices in the flour, then dip in the egg, then coat in the breadcrumbs and place on baking tray. Drizzle over the olive oil. Bake for 7 minutes, then flip slices over and bake for further 8 minutes.

FISH

Omega-3 fats are a great gift that fish give to the world, and then there is the list of other good things: vitamin B12, zinc and the mineral selenium, which is an antioxidant. Antioxidants — and you might hear that term bandied about in health-food circles — are agents that are thought to limit the damage from 'free radicals' in the body thereby protecting against disease. Most of the fish in the sea provide healthy food choices for lucky humans, but some more than others. Two servings a week of oily fish like salmon, sardines, herring, mackerel and trout can keep brains and hearts healthy.

FIVE SUPER FISH

SALMON: Salmon is a queen of the sea and the kitchen. The pink, silky fish is pumping with omega-3 fats. To get your fix, stir salmon chunks into pasta or salad with red onion and spinach leaves and that's dinner. There is one caveat: salmon is a bigger fish and more susceptible to absorbing the high levels of mercury in today's oceans. Mercury is risky especially for pregnant women and young children. Limit servings to two per week.

RAINBOW TROUT: This versatile, fleshy fish tastes like the ocean but never tastes too fishy. Rainbow trout is super-high in omega-3s as well as vitamin B12 and niacin, which is great for balancing cholesterol and the metabolism. Grill it whole with the skin on and you might feel the energy boost for days. Use capers, lemon and maybe some dill as a seasoning. Trout is also delicious and healthy when smoked and tossed in a salad.

TUNA: Barbecued, seared, tinned, or raw and rolled into sushi, tuna is high in the 'good' fats. Grill up a tuna steak with dollops of guacamole; buy tuna in chunks and use as the base for a burger pattie. Just take care: tuna is a big fish like salmon and can carry mercury. Limit servings to two per week.

ANCHOVIES: Not everyone appreciates these salty, chewy gems, but if you love 'em you're lucky. Anchovies are tiny and intense and just a few stirred into a salad dressing or topped on a pizza give the heart and bones an essential boost. Anchovies are bursting with iron, omega-3s, magnesium, calcium and phosphorus. Choose those preserved in olive oil for the best fat option.

OYSTERS: Learn to love oysters. They are one of the healthiest, safest seafoods. Oysters are not known to absorb mercury and are bursting with omega-3s and zinc, which builds up immunity and gives lots of energy. Eat them raw with lemon, or grill and sprinkle with bacon for a luxurious treat.

Fresh Fish Tacos with Yoghurt Dressing

GET THE PARTY STARTED WITH THESE VIBRANT, CRUNCHY, FLAVOUR-FILLED MEXICAN TACOS

SERVES 6

MARINADE

¹/₃ cup (80ml, 3fl oz) olive oil

2 limes, juiced

1 clove garlic, minced

1 tbsp smoked paprika

1 tbsp cayenne pepper

6 white fish fillets, cut into large chunks (such as snapper or blue eye)

Olive oil, for brushing

DRESSING

1 cup (250g, 8oz) mayonnaise

½ cup (125g, 4oz) sour cream

1 tbsp fresh coriander, finely chopped

1 clove garlic, minced

Pinch of salt and pepper

TO SERVE

12 tortillas

1 butter lettuce, leaves torn

20 cherry tomatoes, quartered

½ head radicchio, shredded

1 cup (20g, ¾ oz) packed coriander leaves

½ cup (60g, 2oz) tasty cheese, grated

½ lime, juiced

1 lime, cut into 6 wedges

Combine the marinade ingredients in a small mixing bowl and whisk to combine.

Put the fish in a sealable bag and add the marinade. Turn gently to coat the fish in the marinade. Set aside to marinate in the bag for 30 minutes.

Whisk together mayonnaise, sour cream, coriander and garlic in a large bowl. Season with salt and pepper. Cover the bowl with plastic wrap and refrigerate for 30 minutes.

Preheat the grill to a high heat.

Remove the fish from the marinade, rinse and pat each fillet dry with a paper towel.

Brush both sides of the fish lightly with oil. Put the fish on the grill and cook for 5 minutes, turning once.

Move the fish to a warm platter, drizzle with lime juice, and cover with aluminium foil or a plate to keep warm.

Quickly warm each tortilla on the grill. To serve, place some lettuce, tomato, radicchio, coriander and cheese in the tortillas, top with fish and garnish with dressing and lime wedges.

Risotto with Smoked Fish

SMOKY HADDOCK GIVES THIS DELICIOUSLY CREAMY
RISOTTO A PROTEIN AND OMEGA-3 BOOST

SERVES 4

3 tbsps olive oil

2 cloves garlic, crushed

3 medium leeks, sliced

300g (10oz) risotto rice
(Arborio or carnaroli)

2 bay leaves

4 cups (1L, 2pt) hot
vegetable stock

200g (7oz) light cream
cheese, at room
temperature

½ cup (125g, 4oz) Greek
yoghurt

100g (3½ oz) baby
spinach leaves

350g (12oz) smoked
haddock fillets (or
smoked cod or snapper
fillets)

60g (2oz) Parmesan
cheese, grated

Fresh lemon juice, to
taste

Sea salt and freshly
ground black pepper

Heat 2 tablespoons of the olive oil in a large frying pan with high sides over medium heat. Add the garlic and leeks and saute for 10 minutes until the leek has softened.

Add the rest of the olive oil and the rice and stir for 1 minute until the rice is translucent.

Add the bay leaves and add the vegetable stock, a third of a cup at a time, stirring it into the rice until all the liquid is absorbed before adding the next batch of stock. This should take about 20 minutes.

Stir through the cream cheese and yoghurt along with the spinach leaves for 5 minutes until the spinach has softened.

Break up the haddock into bite-sized pieces, removing as many bones as you can, and gently stir it into the risotto. Turn the heat to low and let it gently heat through for 5 minutes.

Add lemon juice and season to taste.

Stir through half the Parmesan and serve with the rest of the Parmesan sprinkled over.

Mediterranean Baked Trout

A BEAUTIFULLY LIGHT DISH THAT COMBINES THE FRESH FLAVOURS
OF THE OCEAN WITH EARTHY HERBS AND BALASMIC VINEGAR

SERVES 2

2 rainbow trout fillets

200g (7oz) cherry
tomatoes, quartered

Juice of ½ lemon

2 tbsps balsamic
vinegar

1 tsp olive oil

2 tbsps fresh
rosemary leaves

Salt and pepper

½ lemon, cut into
wedges

Preheat the oven to 200°C (400°F, Gas Mark 6).

Take two large pieces of baking paper and fold both in half.

Place the tomatoes on one side of each piece of paper.

Place a piece of fish over the top and then sprinkle over the
lemon juice, balsamic vinegar, olive oil and rosemary leaves.

Fold the paper over the stacked veggies and fish. From the
top corner, fold the edge over and crease with your fingernail.
Continue to fold and crease all the way around until you have a
sealed pocket.

Place in the oven and bake for 15 minutes on a rimmed
baking tray.

Serve with salt and pepper and a wedge of lemon.

Edamame & Parsley Salad

SERVES 4

3 tbsps flaxseed oil

1 small onion, diced

2 cups (350g, 12oz) shelled and cooked edamame

2 cloves garlic, crushed

½ tbsp soy sauce

1 tbsp apple cider vinegar

¾ cup (35g, 1¼ oz) fresh parsley leaves, roughly chopped

Salt and pepper

Heat 1 tablespoon of the oil in a medium frying pan over medium heat. Fry the onion and garlic for 5 minutes, until the onion is softened. Turn the heat up to medium-high and add the edamame beans.

Saute them for 4 minutes until some are slightly golden.

Remove from the pan and place in a large bowl. Gently toss the beans together with the rest of the ingredients.

Season to taste and serve.

Broad Bean & Barley Salad

SERVES 4

4 cups (1L, 2pt) vegetable stock

500g (1lb 2oz) fresh broad beans, shelled

225g (8oz) pearl barley

1 cup (45g, 1½ oz) fresh mint leaves, roughly chopped

1 bunch small radishes, quartered

1 clove garlic, minced

120g (4oz) toasted hazelnuts, roughly chopped

150g (5oz) Greek feta

DRESSING

4 tbsps flaxseed oil

1 tbsp red wine vinegar

1 tbsp finely chopped mint

Bring stock to a boil in a large pot. Boil broad beans for 2 minutes until tender. Remove with slotted spoon. Rinse in cold water, place in large bowl and set aside. Add barley to the stock, reduce heat to low and simmer, covered, for 40 minutes until tender. Drain and add to the bowl with the beans. Stir through the mint leaves, radishes, garlic and hazelnuts. Whisk all the dressing ingredients together and pour over the salad mix. Season to taste. Serve with crumbled feta.

EDAMAME

These cute little beans are the easiest snack ever. Buy them frozen (preferably organic), steam them, salt them, then start snacking. Edamame are young soybeans served still in the pod. In Japanese restaurants they come steaming in a covered bowl, usually seasoned with sea salt that enhances the buttery flavour. The beans are packed with protein and contain just enough fat to satisfy for a few hours. They can also be taken out of their pods and pureed with lemon, salt and light vegetable oil, then smeared over a tuna steak.

Spicy Calamari in Tomato Sauce

A JUICY, SUCCULENT, TAPAS-STYLE DISH THAT'S EASY TO CREATE AT HOME

SERVES 4

TOMATO SAUCE

2 tbsps olive oil

½ small red onion, diced

2 cloves garlic, crushed

½ small carrot, grated

1 x 400g (14oz) can crushed tomatoes

¼ cup (60ml, 2fl oz) vegetable stock

1 tbsp fresh oregano leaves, chopped

Salt and freshly ground pepper

CALAMARI

2 tbsps olive oil

3 cloves garlic, crushed

1 large onion, chopped

450g (1oz) green beans

2 tsps chilli flakes

450g (1lb) calamari rings

1 cup (225g, 8oz) tomato sauce

½ cup (125ml, 4fl oz) dry white wine (such as sauvignon blanc)

Salt and freshly ground pepper

First make the tomato sauce. Heat the olive oil in a medium saucepan over medium-high heat. Saute the onion and garlic for 5 minutes, until the onion has softened. Add the carrot, tomatoes and stock and bring to the boil. Reduce the heat to low and simmer, covered, for 40 minutes, until the sauce has thickened. Uncover and add the oregano. Cook for a further 10 minutes. Season to taste and set aside.

Now prepare the calamari. In a large frying pan, heat the olive oil over medium-high heat. Add the garlic and onion and saute for 5 minutes. Add the beans and chilli and cook for a further 4 minutes.

Add the calamari rings, the tomato sauce you made earlier, and the white wine. Quickly bring to a boil and then reduce the heat to low. Simmer for 1 minute, or until the calamari are cooked.

Serve with some extra olive oil drizzled over and season to taste.

Coconut Chicken Noodle Bowl

PEANUTS FOR PROTEIN, NOODLES FOR ENERGY, VEGGIES FOR CRUNCH AND HERBS FOR FLAVOUR: THIS BOWL OF GOODNESS HAS IT ALL

SERVES 4

300g (10oz) rice vermicelli noodles

½ tsp sesame oil

2 large chicken breast fillets, skin removed

3 tbsps fresh ginger, minced

1 stalk lemongrass, white part only, roughly chopped

2 limes, zested and juiced

¾ cup (200ml, 7fl oz) coconut milk

¾ cup (200ml, 7fl oz) vegetable stock

½ wombok (Chinese cabbage), shredded

1 carrot, finely julienned

1 cup (100g, 4oz) bean sprouts, rinsed

1 cup (140g, 5oz) green papaya, finely julienned

1 cup (45g, 1½ oz) fresh coriander leaves, roughly chopped

2 tbsps brown sugar

2 tbsps fish sauce

1 long red chilli, seeds removed, thinly sliced

¾ cup (90g, 3oz) roasted peanuts, coarsely chopped

Bring a pot of water to the boil and cook the vermicelli noodles according to the instructions. Drain and stir through the sesame oil to prevent it sticking, and set aside.

Place the chicken fillets, 2 tablespoons ginger, lemongrass, the lime zest and half the lime juice, coconut milk and stock in a medium saucepan over high heat and bring to a boil.

Immediately reduce the heat to low and simmer the chicken for 5 minutes, covered. Turn off the heat and leave the chicken to poach for 30 minutes. Remove the chicken from the broth and place in the fridge in a covered container to let it cool completely for at least 1 hour.

Shred the chicken into a large mixing bowl. Add the cabbage, carrot, sprouts, papaya and coriander.

In a small bowl, whisk together the rest of the lime juice and ginger, brown sugar and fish sauce. Pour over the salad ingredients and toss to combine.

To serve, top the noodles with the salad and sprinkle over the chilli and peanuts.

Steamed Ginger Chicken

IF YOU'VE OVERINDULGED A BIT TODAY, HERE'S A LIGHT
AND HEALTHY DINNER OPTION FOR TONIGHT

SERVES 4

4 chicken breast fillets, skin removed

½ cup (125ml, 4fl oz) light soy sauce

½ tsp five-spice powder

¼ cup (60ml, 2fl oz) Shaoxing rice wine

2 tbsps fresh ginger, minced

2 tsps lemon zest

1 tbsp palm sugar (or brown sugar)

Salt and pepper

1 sprig fresh rosemary, for garnish

In a small bowl, mix together the soy sauce, five-spice powder, rice wine, ginger, lemon zest and sugar.

Pour the sauce over the chicken fillets and set them aside to marinate in the fridge for at least 30 minutes.

Fit the chicken breasts in a large steamer basket. Bring at least 3cm (1in) of water to boil under the steamer basket.

Cover the basket and steam the breast fillets for 12 minutes, or until the breasts are cooked through. Let them sit for 2 minutes.

In a small saucepan, bring the remaining marinade sauce to a boil.

Serve the chicken breasts with the sauce poured over and a couple of rosemary leaves sprinkled as garnish.

Beef Sirloin with Horseradish Cream Sauce

PERFECTLY COOKED STEAK AND PEPPERY HORSERADISH ONLY
NEED A SIMPLE SALAD AND THAT'S DINNER DONE

SERVES 2

1 tsp olive oil

2 x 200g (7oz) fillet steak (eye fillet or sirloin steak)

Salt and pepper

2 cups (60g, 2oz) fresh rocket leaves, rinsed and dried

½ pear, thinly sliced

1 tbsp olive oil

1 tsp balsamic vinegar

50g (2oz) shaved Parmesan cheese

HORSERADISH CREAM SAUCE

½ cup (125g, 4oz) Greek yoghurt

½ tsp tomato sauce

2 tsps Dijon mustard

2 tbsps grated horseradish

1 tsp apple cider vinegar

Pinch of salt and pepper

Heat a large grill pan to high heat until it's smoking.

Lightly brush the steaks with olive oil and season with salt and pepper.

Place the steaks on the grill pan — try not to let the steaks touch each other. Give them space.

Cook the steaks for 2 minutes on each side for medium-rare. (Don't turn them more than once.)

Once cooked, let the steaks sit on a warming plate for 3 minutes before serving. This helps them stay moist.

To make the sauce, whisk all the sauce ingredients together in a small bowl. Season to taste with the salt and pepper.

To make the salad, mix together the rocket and pear with the olive oil and balsamic vinegar and season with salt and pepper. Gently mix through the Parmesan.

Serve the steaks with the salad and sauce.

Pan-Seared Duck Breast

TENDER JUICY DUCK BREAST WITH CRISPY SKIN IS A WORTHWHILE TREAT FOR THE TASTE BUDS

SERVES 2

2 duck breasts, skin on

Zest of ½ orange

½ tsp rosemary, chopped

Salt and freshly ground pepper

1 tbsp honey

Pat dry the duck breasts. Score the skin in a crosshatch pattern. Don't cut it any deeper than the fat.

Rub the zest, rosemary and a good pinch or two of salt and pepper into each breast.

Place the breasts, skin down, in a medium-heavy frying pan while it's still cold.

Heat the pan to medium-high heat.

Cook for 7 minutes, until the skin has become crispy.

Turn the breasts over and drizzle the honey over each breast. Cook for another 4 minutes, until the duck is cooked to your preferred level of tenderness.

Rest the breasts for 3 minutes on a warming plate after you've finished cooking them to keep them moist.

Carve into slices and serve with a side of fresh mixed salad leaves.

Flaxseed Dukkah

MAKES 2 CUPS

½ cup (60g, 2oz) almonds

1 tbsp pine nuts

1 cup (170g, 6oz) flaxseeds

¾ cup (120g, 4oz) sesame seeds

2 tbsps coriander seeds

2 tbsps cumin seeds

3 tbsps fennel seeds

1 tbsp chilli flakes

½ tsp black peppercorns

Salt and pepper, to taste

Preheat oven to 180°C (350°F, Gas Mark 4). Spread all the ingredients out on large flat roasting trays. Roast the almonds and pine nuts for 10 minutes or until they become golden brown. Roast the seeds for 5 minutes.

Place everything in a blender and pulse several times until the dukkah is at your preferred texture. Add salt and pepper to taste.

Store in an airtight container.

Flaxseed Salad & Miso Dressing

SERVES 4

½ butternut pumpkin, cut into 2cm (1in) cubes

3 large beetroots, peeled and cut into large chunks

1 tbsp olive oil

½ tsp each salt and pepper

3 heaped cups (100g, 3½ oz) rocket leaves

2 tbsps flaxseeds

MISO DRESSING

3 tbsps balsamic vinegar

¼ cup (60ml, 2fl oz) walnut oil

2 tbsps lemon juice

2 tsps white miso

1 tsp honey

1 tsp caraway seeds

Preheat oven to 200°C (400°F, Gas Mark 6). Line a baking tray with baking paper. Toss pumpkin and beetroot with the olive oil, salt and pepper, and spread over the tray in one layer. Bake for 50 minutes until tender. Whisk dressing ingredients in a small bowl. Toss the pumpkin and beetroot with the rocket and flaxseeds. Drizzle the dressing over the salad and serve.

FLAXSEEDS

These nutty brown seeds have earned their superfood status. The oil in flaxseeds is packed with omega-3 fats thought to help reduce inflammation, balance hormones (think: mood swings) and prevent heart disease. Two tablespoons a day of the seeds or the oil will do the trick. Buy seeds raw or toasted and throw in salads and soups, or add to a morning smoothie for texture and flavour. Also, experiment with home-made seasonings: grind flaxseeds and add them to blends of salt, poppyseeds or chilli flakes, or go sweet with cinnamon or nutmeg.

QUINOA

Quinoa is a tiny, vibrant little seed that comes in many colours — it is not a grain, as is commonly thought, but a seed (and a gluten-free one too). It grows on tall, grain-like plants that come in bright pinks, purples, white, reds and black. Strangely, the plant is related to spinach.

Quinoa has become a darling of the health-food movement. Its seeds are bigger and crunchier than couscous and they contain all nine of the essential amino acids, which the body uses to energize and heal. And like fish and avocado, quinoa is full of omega-3s that are great for the heart. The colours are sold separately or in a rainbow combination, each ever-so-slightly different in texture and flavour. Quinoa is often used to replace rice and pasta as a healthier carbohydrate high in protein and fibre. When boiled and steamed, quinoa comes out fluffy and a bit crunchy with a subtle nutty taste.

COOK IT LIKE A PRO

- Rinse it well! A good rinse washes off the bitter coating that has formed around the seed to protect it from the elements.
- Like rice, quinoa is easy to cook once a technique is mastered. Cook it just enough to soften, so it's easily digestible, though avoid the mushiness of overcooking. A reliable method: bring 1 cup of quinoa in 2 cups of water to a boil. Reduce the heat to very low, then cover and simmer for 15 minutes until grains are tender. Let sit for a further 5 minutes, off the heat but still covered, then fluff with a fork before serving.

SERVING TIPS

- Quinoa absorbs flavours well. Lemon, chives and dill are excellent seasonings as the seed supports their pungent flavour.
- Due to quinoa's softness, the crunchy textures of vegetables and nuts are a great complement.
- Quinoa and salads go hand in hand. Creamy feta cheese and spinach is a lovely combination, or simply experiment for yourself.
- Quinoa burgers are a vegetarian delight. Cook the quinoa first, then roll into patties along with hearty vegetables like mushrooms, potato and sweet potato.
- Home-made 'quinoa bars' are a creative alternative to muesli bars and protein bars that can be packed with sugar and hidden ingredients. The sweetness can come instead from fresh and dried fruits — perhaps apples, apricots, sultanas or cherries. Sunflower seeds and crushed nuts add so much oomph.

Quick Quinoa and Pork Meatballs

THE BREADCRUMBS THAT OFTEN FEATURE IN MEATBALLS ARE REPLACED WITH QUINOA IN THIS CRUNCHY, FRESH AND GLUTEN-FREE DINNER

SERVES 4

MEATBALLS

¾ cup (130g, 4oz) uncooked quinoa

1½ cups (375ml, 13fl oz) vegetable stock

450g (1lb) pork mince

3 spring onions, finely chopped

3 cloves garlic, crushed

2 eggs, lightly beaten

½ tsp freshly ground pepper

½ tsp chilli powder

½ tbsp dried mixed herbs

¼ tsp salt

Freshly ground pepper

¼ cup (40g, 1½ oz) sesame seeds

1 tbsp flaxseeds

SALAD

3 stalks celery, sliced

3 Lebanese cucumbers, chopped

150g (5oz) mixed lettuce leaves

12 cherry tomatoes, quartered

1 pomegranate, seeded

4 radishes, thinly sliced

¼ cup (60g, 2oz) walnuts, roughly chopped

2 tbsps olive oil

1 lime, cut into wedges

Preheat oven to 230°C (450°F, Gas Mark 8). Line a large flat baking tray with baking paper.

Rinse the quinoa and put into a medium saucepan with the stock. Bring to a boil, then reduce the heat to low, cover and cook for 15 minutes or until the quinoa is cooked. Stir occasionally to ensure the quinoa isn't sticking to the bottom of the pot. Transfer the quinoa to a large mixing bowl and let cool for 15 minutes.

Add the rest of the ingredients, except the sesame and flaxseeds, and mix together until thoroughly combined.

Shape about 2 tablespoons of the mixture into meatballs.

Mix the sesame and flaxseeds in a shallow dish.

Roll each meatball in the sesame and flaxseeds and place on the baking tray.

Bake for 7 minutes, turn them over and bake for a further 8 minutes or until they're golden brown.

To make the salad toss all the salad ingredients together in a bowl.

Serve the warm meatballs with the salad. Sprinkle over some sesame seeds to garnish, and add lime wedges on the side.

Kale and Quinoa Salad

QUINOA AND KALE: TWO SUPERFOODS IN ONE MEAL.
THIS SALAD IS SURE TO GET YOU UP AND AT 'EM

SERVES 4

1 cup (170g, 6oz)
uncooked quinoa

½ cup (90g, 3oz) brown
lentils

5 cups (1.25L, 2pt
10fl oz) vegetable stock

¼ cup (60ml, 2fl oz)
olive oil

2 bunches broccolini,
cut into small pieces

2 bunches kale,
chopped

12 cherry tomatoes,
quartered

2 x 400g (14oz) can
four-bean mix, drained
and rinsed

¼ cup (60ml, 2fl oz)
lemon juice

2 tsps balsamic vinegar

Salt and pepper

Rinse the quinoa and lentils and place in a large saucepan with
the stock. Bring to a boil, then reduce the heat to low, cover and
cook for 15 minutes or until the quinoa and lentils are cooked.
Stir occasionally to ensure nothing is sticking to the bottom of
the pot. Drain and rinse the quinoa and lentils and set aside in a
large mixing bowl.

Heat 2 tablespoons of the olive oil in a large frying pan over
medium-high heat.

Stir-fry the broccolini for 6 minutes until it starts to brown.

Add the kale and fry for a further 2 minutes.

Add the tomatoes and gently stir through for 1 minute.

Add the broccolini, kale and tomatoes to the quinoa and lentils.
Add the four-bean mix and the rest of the ingredients. Toss
everything together to mix thoroughly.

Season to taste and serve.

Dairy Free

NUT MILK

Health-food aisles and cafe menus are bursting with so many healthy alternatives to milk, it's possible to drink a different milk every day of the week. And lactose-free people need not suffer without the indulgence of 'dairy'. The most popular option is almond milk, which is essentially a bunch of almonds soaked overnight, then blended with warm water to get a fine, silky fluid. This is strained and voila: nut milk. It's easy to do at home! Experiment with walnuts, brazil nuts, cashews, pistachios and pecans. Use boiling water first to remove the nuts' skins.

NUT MILK TREATS

- GOLDEN MILK: Caffeine-free and full of goodness, the yellow-gold wonder spice turmeric gives this soothing drink its name. Turmeric has been consumed for generations in India, where it's considered a tonic for everything from colds and joint pain to skin blemishes. Splurge at a local cafe, then try to recreate it at home: blend ginger, nutmeg, pepper, raw honey and cardamom with coconut milk. Warm, then froth it like a latte and sprinkle with cinnamon.
- TEAS: Use tea instead of water when making nut milks. English Breakfast tea, Earl Grey tea, peppermint tea or chamomile tea are especially delicious. These infuse the milk with delicate flavours. Pour over cereal or porridge and it's like a cup of tea and breakfast bowl all in one.
- CHOCOLATE NUT MILK: Heat cocoa powder and simple syrup made with brown sugar, then stir into nut milk and there's a dairy-free chocolate milk. Or experiment: vanilla, medjool dates (voluptuous, creamy dates that taste like caramel plucked from a tree), cocoa, cinnamon and a pinch of salt makes a richer, sweeter beverage.
- BANANA NUT 'ICE CREAM': This is part smoothie, part soft-serve ice cream. Throw almond milk in a blender with frozen bananas, honey and crystallized ginger. Whizz just enough to make creamy, yet stay icy. Sprinkle with cinnamon or spoon onto a bowl of raspberries.

TWO SAVOURY DISHES

- CAULIFLOWER PUREE: Boil cauliflower until just before it's soft. Add to blender with almond milk and nutmeg, or pepper, and process until soft and creamy. Add Parmesan cheese to taste.
- CREAMED SPINACH: Use almond milk to make a version of the classic white bechamel sauce. Pour the white sauce over spinach and maybe sprinkle with grated Parmesan. Top with slivered almonds and bake until golden brown.

Almond Chocolate Milk

DAIRY-FREE DOESN'T MEAN MISSING OUT, ON THE GOOD STUFF.
THIS CHOCOLATE MILK IS PROOF POSITIVE

SERVES 4-6

1½ cups (185g, 6oz) raw almonds

6 cups (1.5L, 3pt 3fl oz) filtered water

1 tsp vanilla extract

Pinch of sea salt flakes

1 cup (175g, 6oz) dark chocolate, chopped, or ¼ cup (30g, 1oz) cacao powder and 3 dates

Place the almonds in a bowl and cover with 2½ cups of the filtered water. Soak for 12 to 24 hours.

Drain and rinse the almonds.

Add them to a blender with the rest of the filtered water along with the vanilla, salt and chocolate (or cacao powder and dates).

Blend on high for 2 minutes.

Pour the blended mixture into a straining bag, such as a nut milk bag or cheesecloth bag, and let it drain into a large bowl for 1½ hours.

Squeeze any remaining liquid out into the bowl. Discard the mixture in the bag.

Enjoy the milk cold or heated like hot chocolate.

Macadamia Nut Cheese

DAIRY - FREE? YOU DON'T NEED TO MISS OUT ON SMOOTH, CREAMY CHEESES LIKE THIS ONE

SERVES 8

2 cups (250g, 8oz)
raw macadamias

½ tsp salt

2 tsps nutritional yeast

1 tsp probiotic powder

1 tsp lemon juice

½ cup (60g, 2oz)
walnuts

Place the macadamia nuts in a bowl and cover with water. Cover and set aside to soak for 6 hours or overnight. Drain and rinse.

Place macadamias in a high-speed blender and process until very smooth.

Line a colander with cheesecloth and place on top of a plate.

Scrape the mixture into the colander and fold the cloth over the top. Place a weight on top (jars filled with water will do), just heavy enough to apply pressure but not to push the mixture through the cloth.

Set aside at room temperature for 24 to 48 hours.

Add the salt, nutritional yeast, probiotic powder and lemon juice to the macadamias and stir to combine.

Scrape the mixture into a cheese mould or plastic container. Transfer to the freezer for 3 to 4 hours.

Serve with walnut pieces pressed into the top, arranged around the rim pointing towards the middle.

Notes: To create a rind, the cheese can be placed in a dehydrator at 43°C (110°F) for 24 hours after freezing.

Cashew nuts may be used in place of macadamia nuts in this recipe.

Store in an airtight container in the fridge for 5 to 7 days.

Dairy-Free Blueberry and Cacao Ice Cream

BRIGHT, COLOURFUL, CREAMY AND SO EASY TO MAKE
— THAT'S SUMMER SORTED

SERVES 4–5

BLUEBERRY ICE CREAM

2 cups (400g, 14oz) frozen banana slices

2 cups (200g, 7oz) frozen blueberries

4 tbsps almond milk

CACAO ICE CREAM

125g (4oz) silken tofu

$1/3$ cup (115g, 4oz) maple syrup

$1/3$ cup (45g, 1½ oz) cacao powder

½ cup (125ml, 4fl oz) coconut cream

1 cup (250ml, 8fl oz) almond milk

1 tsp vanilla extract

BLUEBERRY ICE CREAM

Let the frozen banana and blueberries defrost for 5 minutes.

Place everything into a blender and pulse a couple of times to break the fruit up.

Then blend until the mixture achieves a thick pureed ice-cream consistency.

Serve immediately or freeze overnight.

CACAO ICE CREAM

Place the tofu and maple syrup in a blender and blend until thoroughly combined.

Add the cacao, coconut cream, almond milk and vanilla extract and blend for 1 minute until everything is thoroughly combined.

Pour into an ice-cream container and place in the freezer to set for at least 4 hours, preferably overnight.

Paleo Chocolate Mousse

SERVES 4

2 large ripe avocados

½ cup (125ml, 4fl oz) coconut cream, chilled

¼ cup (30g, 1oz) cacao powder

1 tsp ground flaxseeds

3 tsps maple syrup

1 tsp vanilla extract

¼ tsp ground cardamom

¼ cup (30g, 1oz) toasted hazelnuts, finely chopped, reserve 1 tbsp for garnish

Pinch of sea salt

4 sprigs mint, to garnish

Place all ingredients except the garnish in a blender.

Blend until everything is a thick puree.

Spoon the mousse into serving dishes.

Chill in the fridge for at least 3 hours before serving.

Serve sprinkled with chopped hazelnuts and a sprig of mint.

Detox Green Smoothie

SERVES 2

120g (4oz) fresh baby spinach leaves

1 orange, peeled

1 kiwi fruit, peeled

2 stalks celery

½ cup (70g, 2½ oz) honeydew melon, chopped

3 sprigs fresh mint, leaves removed

1 tsp fresh ginger, minced

Place all the ingredients into a blender.

Blend for at least 2 minutes, until everything is a smooth puree.

Pour into individual serving glasses and serve.

Keep any unused drink chilled and stir before drinking.

HAZELNUTS

Hazelnuts are a bit of a star in the dessert world. Buttery and mildly salty, they blend and morph with powerful flavours like chocolate and vanilla and add a rich crunch when mixed with berries and citrus fruits. They can be ground with the bright brown skin still on and churned into a chocolate mousse without any chocolate…and it will taste chocolatey. (Cocoa powder, maple syrup and vanilla do help with this!) Hazelnuts blend beautifully with anything creamy, whether dairy or dairy-free. Blend them with coconut milk and there'll be a naturally sweet, earthy smoothie pumping with protein.

Raw Chocolate Mousse Cake with Chocolate Sauce

THIS DECADENT DESSERT IS A PERFECT CHOICE FOR A SPECIAL DINNER WITH FRIENDS AND FAMILY

SERVES 10

CRUST

½ cup (60g, 2oz) almonds

½ cup (60g, 2oz) cashews

1 cup (90g, 3oz) desiccated coconut

1 cup (175g, 6oz) pitted dates, soaked in water for 15 minutes

½ tsp vanilla extract

2 tbsps raw cacao powder (or unsweetened cocoa)

FILLING

¾ cup (185ml, 6fl oz) coconut milk

250g (9oz) silken tofu

1 cup (110g, 4oz) raw cacao powder (or unsweetened cocoa)

2 tbsps ground flaxseeds

¼ cup (90g, 3oz) maple syrup

3 large ripe avocados

1 cup (175g, 6oz) pitted dates, soaked in ¼ cup water

1 tbsp cashew butter

1 tsp coconut oil

CHOCOLATE SAUCE

½ cup (125ml, 4fl oz) coconut oil

½ cup (60g, 2oz) cocoa powder

½ cup (60g, 2oz) maple syrup

Pinch of sea salt

½ cup (60g, 2oz) cashew halves, to decorate

To make the crust, place the nuts in a blender and pulse a few times until they're roughly chopped. Add the rest of the crust ingredients and pulse a couple more times until you have a rough, sticky meal.

Grease a 23 x 4cm (9 x 1.5in) pie dish. Press the crust mix into the dish and about 3cm (1in) up the sides.

Place into the freezer to chill for at least 1 hour.

To make the filling, place all the ingredients into a blender and blend for 2 minutes or until you have a smooth puree.

Pour the filling into the pie dish and place in the freezer.

Chill for 4 hours if you like a creamy filling or overnight if you want a hard filling. But let it warm for at least 30 minutes before serving if you've chilled it overnight.

To make the sauce gently warm the coconut oil, then whisk in the cocoa, maple syrup and sea salt.

Press the cashew halves into the top of the cake and drizzle with the melted dark chocolate and serve.

Raw Coconut and Berry Cheesecakes

LOW ON SUGAR AND HIGH ON FLAVOUR, THESE LITTLE CHEESECAKES MAKE A LOVELY DESSERT TO SHARE

MAKES 12

3 cups (375g, 13oz) cashews

¾ cup (185ml, 6fl oz) lemon juice

¾ cup (260g, 9oz) honey

¾ cup (185ml, 6fl oz) coconut oil

2 cups (250g, 8oz) raspberries, frozen

1 tbsp vanilla extract

Water, as required

1 cup (200g, 7oz) mixed berries, frozen, to decorate

Line a 12-hole muffin or cupcake tin with cupcake cases.

Place all ingredients except the mixed berries into a blender and pulse to loosen up the ingredients. Then blend for 1 minute or until you have a smooth puree, adding water only if needed to loosen the mixture for blending.

Pour the berry mixture in the cupcake cases in equal portions.

Place in the freezer for at least 4 hours, preferably overnight.

Let the cheesecakes defrost for 30 minutes before serving.

Remove the cupcake cases and decorate with frozen mixed berries to serve.

Lemon Coconut Bars

TANGY LEMON AND A CRISPY CRUST: THESE BARS HAVE ALL THE
MAKINGS OF A 'YOU CAN COME AGAIN' AFTERNOON SNACK

SERVES 4

BASE

¾ cup (260g, 9oz)
honey

½ cup (125ml, 4fl oz)
coconut oil, room
temperature

Pinch of salt

¾ cup (60g, 2oz)
desiccated coconut

1 cup (125g, 4oz)
coconut flour, sifted

FILLING

3 eggs

½ cup (180g, 6oz)
honey

Zest of 1 lemon

2 tsps coconut flour

Juice of 3 lemons

Preheat oven to 175°C (350°F, Gas Mark 4). Grease a rectangular
baking tin.

In an electric mixer, beat together honey, coconut oil and
salt until creamy. Add desiccated coconut and mix until well
combined.

Fold in coconut flour until a soft dough forms.

Press dough into the cake tin. Place in the oven and bake for
8 minutes, until golden brown. Remove from oven and allow to
cool for 30 minutes.

Lower oven temperature to 160°C (320°F, Gas Mark 3).

In a clean bowl, using the electric mixer whisk the eggs, honey
and lemon zest together.

In another bowl, combine the coconut flour and lemon juice.

Add the egg mixture into the flour mixture and fold to
incorporate.

Pour lemon filling over the baked crust and return to the oven to
bake for 20 minutes, until set.

Remove from oven and set aside to cool partially. Cover and
refrigerate for 6 hours. When chilled, slice into bars.

Creamy Peanut Butter

MAKES 1 CUP

1 cup (125g, 4oz) raw peanuts (unsalted and unsoaked)

1 cup (125g, 4oz) raw cashews (unsalted and unsoaked)

½ tsp sea salt

2 tbsps honey (optional)

Place the nuts into the bowl of a food processer.

Process for 5 minutes, stopping occasionally to scrape the bowl down, until a powder forms.

Continue processing the nuts for a further 15 minutes. During this time, the butter will first form a dough-like consistency, then appear whipped before forming a buttery consistency.

Add salt and honey, if using, and stir until combined.

Transfer butter to a jar and store in the fridge.

Peanut Butter Smoothie

SERVES 1–2

2 bananas

1 cup (250ml, 8fl oz) soy milk

1 frozen banana

½ cup (40g, 1½ oz) rolled oats, uncooked (plus extra to garnish)

¼ cup (60g, 2oz) natural peanut butter

1 tsp cinnamon

1 cup (150g, 5oz) ice cubes

Add all the ingredients to the blender and process until smooth enough to drink.

Add more milk if required to reach desired consistency.

Pour into glasses, garnish with oats and serve immediately.

PEANUTS

There's a reason peanut butter is such a staple: it's energy in a jar. Peanuts are not nuts, they are legumes, which means a seed that grows in a pod. Peanuts get a bad rap — allergies are common, and can be severe. Although peanuts have a high fat content for such little things, it's mostly the 'good' fat and studies show that diets high in peanuts are low in heart-related diseases. Raw peanuts are the best choice — skip the salt, sugar and extra oil that often comes with the roasted and packaged brands.

Ginger Biscuits

GLUTEN-FREE AND DAIRY-FREE, THESE CRISPY, TASTY BISCUITS ARE A SAFE CHOICE FOR KIDS' LUNCHBOXES OR PARTIES

125g (4oz) dairy-free butter or margarine

¼ cup (90g, 3oz) golden syrup

¹/₃ cup (115g, 4oz) maple syrup

2½ cups (310g, 10oz) plain gluten-free flour

1½ tbsps ground ginger

1 tbsp fresh ginger, minced

1 tsp bicarbonate of soda

1 tsp ground cinnamon

¼ tsp baking powder

1 tbsp ground flaxseeds, combined with 3 tbsps water

¼ cup (60ml, 2fl oz) water

Preheat oven to 180°C (350°F, Gas Mark 4). Line a large flat baking tray with baking paper.

Melt the butter together with the golden syrup and maple syrup in a medium saucepan. Remove from heat and set aside.

In a large mixing bowl, mix together the flour, gingers, bicarb, cinnamon and baking powder. Make a well in the centre.

Mix the flaxseed mixture with the butter and syrups and then pour into the mixing bowl. Stir together to form a dough; add the water in small doses if you need it. You may not need all the water.

Roll heaped tablespoons of the dough into small balls and place on the baking tray. Flatten slightly and ensure you leave space between each one as they will spread.

Bake for 15 minutes, until golden.

Reduce the temperature to 140°C (285°F, Gas Mark 1) and bake the biscuits for a further 25 minutes.

Let the biscuits cool for at least 10 minutes before removing them to a wire rack to cool completely.

CALCIUM AND GREENS

An apple a day keeps the doctor away and so does a serving, or three, of greens. Nutritionists recommend three to five servings of calcium a day, which can include yet should not be limited to dairy. Greens are cool, crunchy powerhouses of vitamins, minerals and fibre, and they're also an excellent source of calcium. Calcium keeps bones and teeth strong and pearly white, as television ads for milk have always told children. It's also essential for the heart and blood and helps prevent bone conditions like osteoporosis, especially later in life.

Not all greens are equal — the calcium in some greens is not so easy to absorb as others. It's good to know which are the winners in this department.

BEST GREENS

KALE: The vibrant green veggie deserves its glory. Kale has slightly more calcium (as well as vitamin B6) in it than cabbage, Brussels sprouts and spinach. There are lots of varieties, some flecked with red and most with sturdy, frilly green leaves that are great roasted and transformed into kale chips.

SILVERBEET: Also known as Swiss chard, this tall, billowy green vegetable has gently frilled leaves that burst off long white or red stems. The calcium is mostly contained in the leaves, which are mild and earthy flavoured, though the stems are good to eat too.

BROCCOLI: These 'little trees' are related to kale and full of goodness whether eaten raw, steamed or pureed into a soup with a little cream — for added calcium!

BOK CHOY: This Asian green is beloved all over the world. 'Baby' bok choy has elegant, soft, lime-coloured leaves and is delicious steamed with minced ginger and oyster sauce. The mature bok choy is darker green with long white stems; it has a more peppery, pungent flavour.

MUSTARD GREENS: The Asian name for this sharp-flavoured green veggie is 'gai choy'. The leaves are lightly frilled and a bright grass colour that matches the stems. Steam or saute with oil and maybe some ginger and lemongrass for a zesty touch.

COOKING TIP

Blanching greens is a beautiful way to hold the calcium in the veggies before freezing or sauteing. Wash greens while bringing a pot of water to the boil. Throw the greens in the boiling water for 1 minute, then remove and run under cold water to stop the cooking process.

Spaghetti with Pesto and Toasted Almond Flakes

A SIMPLE PASTA DINNER THAT'S GREAT FOR THOSE EVENINGS WHEN YOU JUST NEED TO RELAX AND REFUEL

SERVES 4

1 cup (125g, 4oz) almonds

2 cups (60g, 2oz) fresh spinach, finely chopped, plus extra leaves for garnish

¾ cup (10g, ¼ oz) fresh basil leaves

Salt and pepper, to taste

⅓ cup (80ml, 3fl oz) extra virgin olive oil

455g (1lb) spaghetti

Toasted almond flakes, to serve

Warm a frying pan and dry-roast almonds until golden. Remove from heat and place on paper towels.

Blanch spinach in hot water for 15 seconds, then quickly transfer to an ice bath. Drain and thoroughly pat dry spinach leaves.

Place dried spinach, basil leaves and almonds in a food processer with salt and pepper to taste.

Add oil gradually, until pesto forms a smooth paste.

Bring a large saucepan of salted water to the boil. Add pasta and cook until almost al dente. Drain and set aside.

In a large bowl, mix pesto through spaghetti, until just coated.

Toast the almond flakes in a dry pan over high heat for 2 minutes, until browned.

Serve with toasted almond flakes.

Quinoa Salad with Cranberries and Kale

THIS HEALTHY AND NUTRITIOUS SALAD CAN BE EATEN FOR DINNER OR TAKE IT TO WORK FOR AN ENERGIZING LUNCH

SERVES 8

2 cups (340g, 12oz) uncooked quinoa

4 cups (1L, 2pt) vegetable stock

¾ cup (90g, 3oz) slivered almonds

10 cups (700g, 1½ lb) raw kale, stems removed and chopped

¾ cup (120g, 4oz) dried cranberries

DRESSING

¼ cup (60ml, 2fl oz) lemon juice

1 tsp Dijon mustard

¼ cup (60ml, 2fl oz) olive oil

1 clove garlic, minced

1 tbsp honey

Salt and pepper

Rinse the quinoa and put into a large saucepan with the stock. Bring to a boil, then reduce the heat to low, cover and cook for 15 minutes or until the quinoa is cooked. Stir occasionally to ensure the quinoa isn't sticking to the bottom of the pot.

Once cooked, transfer the quinoa to a large mixing bowl and let cool for 15 minutes.

In a small frying pan, dry-fry the slivered almonds over high heat for 2 minutes or until they start to brown. Add immediately to the quinoa.

Add the kale and cranberries to the bowl and toss everything together.

In a small bowl, vigorously whisk together the dressing ingredients.

Pour the dressing over the salad and toss everything together to thoroughly coat the quinoa and kale.

Season to taste with salt and pepper and serve.

Prawn and Okra Ratatouille

A DELIGHTFULLY VIBRANT AND COLOURFUL DINNER THAT'S FULL OF TEXTURE AND FLAVOUR

SERVES 6

2 tbsps olive oil

3 cloves garlic, minced

1 red onion, halved and sliced

2 tsps ground cumin

2 tsps ground oregano

1 tsp cayenne pepper

2 cups (200g, 7oz) okra, tops removed and cut into 3cm (1in) pieces

1 yellow capsicum, chopped

1 red capsicum, chopped

1 cup (55g, 2oz) semi-dried tomatoes

1²/₃ cups (400ml, 14fl oz) vegetable stock

1 tbsp mixed dried herbs

450g (1lb) raw prawn tails, peeled and deveined

Salt and pepper

2 tsps chilli flakes

Heat the olive oil in a large saucepan over medium-high heat.

Saute the garlic and onion for 4 minutes until the onion is translucent and softened.

Add the cumin, oregano and cayenne pepper and stir for another minute.

Add the okra pieces and cook for 2 minutes.

Add the capsicum and semi-dried tomatoes and fry for another 2 minutes.

Add the stock and the mixed herbs and bring to a boil.

Reduce the heat to low and simmer, covered, for 10 minutes.

Increase the heat back to medium-high then stir through the prawns and cook for 2 minutes, until they are cooked through.

Season to taste and serve garnished with a sprinkling of chilli flakes.

OKRA

Okra are lemony little vegetables with an interesting texture — crunchy at first and then sticky as cooking progresses. Cut off their stems and they are almost geometrical in shape. They come originally from Nigeria where they are known as 'bamia' or ladies' fingers and are used to add a tartness and texture to stews and curries. In India they thicken and brighten vegetable dishes and are eaten fried and spiced as a snack. They are sliced or thrown whole into stir-fries through South East Asia. And in Mediterranean cooking, they are classically stewed up with tomatoes and onions and served as a side dish on a tasting plate.

Okra with Tomatoes

SERVES 2

Oil, for cooking

½ tsp brown mustard seeds

Pinch of asafoetida powder

1 small onion, thinly sliced

1 clove garlic, finely chopped

¼ tsp cumin seeds

Pinch of ground turmeric

1 large tomato, chopped

500g (1lb) okra

¼ tsp chilli powder

1 tsp amchur (dried mango powder)

Fresh basil leaves, to garnish

Salt and pepper, to taste

Heat oil in a frying pan over medium-high heat. Add mustard seeds and cook until they begin to pop. Mix in asafoetida. Reduce heat to low and add onion, garlic, cumin seeds and turmeric. Cook, stirring occasionally, for 5 minutes or until onion is soft and golden brown. Add tomato and okra and stir into the mixture. Gradually mix in chilli powder, amchur, and salt. Cook for 15 minutes, stirring occasionally, until okra is tender but firm.

Roasted Baby Bok Choy

SERVES 4

6 bunches baby bok choy

4 cloves garlic, thickly sliced

2 tbsps olive oil

1 tbsp sesame oil

¼ cup (60ml, 2fl oz) tamari (or soy sauce)

1 tbsp fresh ginger, grated

1 tsp chilli powder

2 tbsps sesame seeds

2 bird's-eye chillies, sliced

Preheat oven to 200°C (400°F, Gas Mark 6). Line a large flat baking tray with baking paper. Cut the bunches of bok choy in half and place in a large bowl and add the garlic slices. In a small bowl, whisk together the olive oil, sesame oil, tamari, ginger, chilli powder and half the sesame seeds. Pour the sauce over the bok choy and toss together to mix the sauce through the bok choy. Lay the bok choy out on the baking tray and pour over any excess sauce from the bowl. Bake in the oven for 8 minutes, until the leaves have begun to wilt. Serve hot, sprinkled with the rest of the sesame seeds and the sliced chilli.

COCONUT MILK

It seems as if the world has gone coconut crazy in recent years. Coconut water is guzzled out of cartons by athletes and the health conscious the world over, as it provides natural electrolytes (like those in sports drinks but without the sugar and obscure additives). Coconut oil is a common substitute for dairy in baking or frying, and coconut milk is the not-so-secret ingredient in many a great curry, scrumptious smoothie and desserts. The creamy, nutty milk has been a saviour for people who are sensitive to lactose.

Coconut milk is made purely from coconut. The beautiful white flesh is grated and soaked in hot water. The coconut cream rises to the top and liquid is squeezed through a cheesecloth to strain the milk. The more straining, the lighter the milk. Thinner coconut milks are used for super-saucy curries. For desserts, a thicker milk is desired, so there might be some cream stirred in.

Coconut milk contains most of the magical health benefits of its source fruit. It's full of fibre, iron and minerals like selenium and magnesium, and it's high in vitamin C and contains crucial B-group vitamins.

There is debate about the fat content of coconut products. Coconut is a high-fat food, some of which is saturated fat. However, it does contain 'medium chain' saturated fats, which can be metabolised more quickly than 'long chain' fats that are in meats and dairy products like cream. Because of this, many weight-loss programs substitute coconut products for vegetable oil, cream, milk and butter. Coconuts are also thought to reduce inflammation and prevent infection. Nutritionists advise the same level of moderation as with dairy products.

COCONUT MILK MEALS

- FOR BREAKFAST: Quinoa porridge becomes a little richer, sweeter and more surprising than the average oats with milk and honey. Add peaches and cinnamon.
- FOR LUNCH: Add a saucy, spicy touch to grilled or sauteed vegetables by tossing in heated coconut milk seasoned with turmeric and ginger.
- FOR DINNER: Rice noodles, vegetables and coconut milk form the basis of a warm, cosy soup.

VARIETIES OF COCONUT MILK

Buy it in a can, or make it at home using unsweetened coconut flakes and water. In a can, opt for the low-fat kind if you are following a weight-loss diet. Regular-fat coconut milk is better for rich, flavourful curries and sauces.

Green Chicken Curry

THIS FRESH THAI CURRY IS AN EASY STAPLE TO
HAVE IN YOUR LIST OF EVERYDAY DINNERS

SERVES 4

1 tsp coconut oil

1 large onion, halved
and sliced

1 x 210ml (7fl oz) can
coconut cream

1½ tbsps green curry
paste

3 chicken breast fillets,
sliced

1 cup (135g, 5oz)
butternut pumpkin, cut
into small slices

350g (12oz) green
beans, ends trimmed,
cut into 4cm (1½ in)
pieces

6-8 kaffir lime leaves,
torn into strips

1 x 400ml (14fl oz) can
coconut milk

1 tbsp fish sauce

1 tbsp palm sugar,
finely chopped

½ cup (10g, ¼ oz) fresh
coriander leaves

Red chilli, sliced, to
serve

Heat the oil in a large work or pan over medium-high heat. Saute
the onion for 5 minutes until translucent and softened.

Pour in the coconut cream and bring to the boil and then reduce
heat. Simmer for 5 minutes or until the cream almost separates.
Stir in the curry paste and cook for a further 2 minutes or until
aromatic.

Add the chicken, pumpkin, beans, kaffir lime leaves and coconut
milk and stir. Reduce to a low heat for 12 minutes, stirring
occasionally, until the chicken is cooked through and the sauce
thickens slightly.

Add the fish sauce, palm sugar and half the coriander to the
curry mixture and stir.

Spoon the curry into bowls and top with the remaining
coriander and sliced red chilli. Serve on top of steamed jasmine
rice, if desired.

Moqueca de Peixe (Brazilian Fish Stew)

THIS FISH STEW IS FULL OF GENTLE, FRAGRANT SPICES AND A RICH SAUCE THAT MAKES FOR A FILLING, DELICIOUS MEAL

SERVES 4

¼ cup (60ml, 2fl oz) olive oil

1 large onion, chopped

4 cloves garlic, minced

1 tbsp ginger, minced

2 tsps chilli powder

1 yellow capsicum, chopped

12 cherry tomatoes, halved

⅓ cup (50g, 2oz) palm hearts, drained, quartered and cut into 3cm (1in) pieces

1 cup (270ml, 9fl oz) coconut milk

2 cups (500ml, 1pt) chicken stock

500g (1lb 2oz) firm white fish fillets, cut into 4cm (1½ in) pieces

500g (1lb 2oz) large prawns, peeled and deveined

500g (1lb 2oz) mussels, scrubbed and debearded

¼ cup (10g, ¼ oz) fresh parsley, chopped

1 lemon, juiced

¼ cup (10g, ¼ oz) fresh coriander leaves, roughly chopped

Heat half the oil in a large saucepan over medium heat. Saute the onion and garlic for 4 minutes until the onion is translucent.

Add the ginger and chilli powder and stir for 1 minute.

Turn the heat up to medium-high and add the rest of the oil, along with the capsicum, tomatoes and palm hearts and stir for 2 minutes.

Add the coconut milk and chicken stock and bring to a boil.

Reduce the heat to low and add the fish. Simmer for 2 minutes, then add the prawns and mussels. Cover and cook for 4 minutes, until the mussels have opened and the prawns are cooked through.

Stir in the parsley, lemon juice and half the coriander leaves.

Serve garnished with the rest of the coriander.

Note: Palm hearts are available in cans, but if you can't find them you can omit from the recipe.

Coconut Ice Cream

VEGAN, DAIRY-FREE AND YOU MIGHT SAY MUCH TASTIER THAN THE STANDARD VARIETY. TRY IT FOR YOURSELF AND SEE

SERVES 6–8

1 x 400ml (14fl oz) can coconut milk

1 x 400ml (14fl oz) can coconut cream

½ cup (180g, 6oz) maple syrup

1½ tsps vanilla extract

½ tsp ground cardamom

¼ tsp salt

2 tbsps cornflour

You will need an ice-cream machine for this recipe.

In a medium saucepan, whisk together the coconut milk, coconut cream, maple syrup, vanilla extract, cardamom and salt.

Mix 3 tablespoons of the coconut liquid in a small glass with the cornflour and set aside.

Heat the ice-cream mixture over medium heat, stirring frequently until the mixture just begins to simmer. Reduce the heat to low and quickly whisk in the cornflour mix (give it a stir before pouring into the ice-cream mix).

Pour the ice-cream mixture into the blender and blend for 30 seconds.

Then pour through a fine-mesh strainer into an airtight container.

Place in the fridge for at least 3 hours to chill.

Pour the mix into your ice-cream machine and churn for 20 minutes or until it has thickened.

Scoop into an airtight ice-cream container. Chill in the freezer for at least 4 hours, preferably overnight.

Serve chilled.

Low Sugar Treats

LOW SUGAR OVERVIEW

Sugar, sugar everywhere. The average Australian, Brit or American consumes around 27 teaspoons of sugar a day, which is 22 more teaspoons than recommended by the World Health Organization. Our brains are intensely receptive to sugar, making it hard to find the off switch. It takes a bit of effort but it is possible to train the taste buds so that processed sugary treats taste like overkill. The goal is to eat so that sugar is barely missed. So, how to wade through the world of low sugar? There are alternatives to satisfy the sweet tooth and ways to focus on the natural sweetness of fresh foods.

A FEW TRICKS

AVOID WHITE SUGAR: The fructose molecule found in refined sugar (and other sugars) is to blame in many chronic problems in the Western world. The body can't process much fructose and it quickly turns to fat in the liver, causing diabetes, heart disease and other health problems.

BUY UNSWEETENED: Look for the unsweetened variations of common foods such as yoghurt, juices and cocoa.

SWITCH CARBOHYDRATES: Shift to wholegrain breads and brown rice. They have higher fibre content and absorb slower than white versions, which promote an insulin-spike response. Look for foods that have at least 3g of fibre per 100 calories.

THE OTHER SUGARS

STEVIA: A herb, processed into a powder or liquid for cooking. It's very sweet, yet it is 100% fructose-free.

ERYTHRITOL: Despite its scientific name, erythritol is a naturally occurring nectar in plants, and fruits and vegetables like grapes and mushrooms.

NATVIA: A natural sweetener made by combining the purest and sweetest parts of the stevia plant and erythritol. Natvia is fructose-free.

COCONUT SUGAR (PICTURED): Coconut sugar is nutritious and causes no sugar high and lows. It does have a fructose content on a par with honey and white sugar, so don't overdo it.

MAPLE SYRUP: The sugary sap from the maple tree is delicious, but it contains about 40% fructose so use in moderation.

RICE MALT SYRUP: Made from boiling brown rice, rice malt syrup (also known as brown rice syrup) is gluten- and wheat-free. It has a mild butterscotch flavour and is 100% fructose-free. Use it on cereal, in drinks and for baking.

Chia Pot with Baked Figs and Honey

A GORGEOUS, HEALTHY DESSERT THAT CAN BE CONSUMED
GUILT - FREE

SERVES 4

CHIA PUDDING

²/₃ cup (160ml, 5fl oz)
coconut cream

2 tbsps honey

Pinch of salt

½ vanilla bean, split
lengthwise and scraped

½ cup (100g, 3oz)
mixed chia seeds

2 cups (500ml, 1pt)
almond milk

FIGS

4 purple figs, halved

1 tbsp coconut oil

2 tbsps honey

¼ tsp vanilla extract

2 tbsps Marsala

Mint leaves, to garnish

Warm coconut cream in a saucepan on low heat. Add honey, salt and vanilla seeds and pod and gently stir for 2 minutes until honey melts.

Remove from heat. Stir in chia seeds and almond milk. Set aside for 5 minutes to allow chia seeds to absorb.

Pour mixture into a jar, cover, and refrigerate for 3 hours.

To bake the figs, preheat the oven to 200°C (400°F, Gas Mark 6).

In a small bowl, stir together the coconut oil, honey and vanilla extract.

Place the figs, skin-side down, in a small baking dish. Drizzle over the honey mixture.

Bake for 20 minutes until soft and starting to caramelise.

Pour the remaining liquid from the tray into a small saucepan and add the Marsala. Bring to the boil and then simmer for 1 minute.

To serve, divide pudding evenly between four serving glasses.

Top each glass with two fig halves and pour over the honey mixture. Garnish with mint leaves.

Raw Coconut Slice with Raspberries

AFTERNOON TEA AT YOUR PLACE? THESE ELEGANT SWEET TREATS
WILL DO THE TRICK

SERVES 8

CRUST

2 cups (250g, 8oz) raw
almonds, pecans or
walnuts

1 cup (175g, 6oz) soft
medjool dates

1 cup (90g, 3oz)
desiccated coconut

1 tsp sea salt

FILLING

3 cups (375g, 13oz) raw
cashews, soaked

3 lemons, juiced

2 tsps vanilla extract

1/3 cup (160ml, 5fl oz)
coconut oil, melted

1/3 cup (230g, 8oz) raw
honey

TOPPING

2 cups (250g, 8oz)
raspberries (fresh or
frozen)

To make the crust, place the nuts, dates, coconut and salt in a
food processor and process until the ingredients hold together
and nuts and fruit have been chopped to the desired consistency.

Scrape the mixture in a mound in the centre of a square or
rectangle springform tin. Press mixture down to form a flat layer.
Place in the fridge while you complete the next step.

Place the filling ingredients in the bowl of a clean food processor
or high-speed blender and process on the highest speed for
3 to 5 minutes until very smooth.

Pour the mixture into the prepared base.

Place raspberries on top of the filling.

Transfer to the freezer for 4 to 6 hours until solid.

Remove from the freezer 30 minutes before eating.

Use a very sharp knife warmed under the hot tap to cut.

NOTE: Store in the freezer.

Blueberry Quinoa Muffins

MAKES 12

2 cups (250g, 8oz) plain flour

1 tsp ground cinnamon

1 tsp bicarbonate of soda

¾ cup (120g, 4oz) firmly packed brown sugar

½ cup (30g, 1oz) quinoa flakes

¾ cup (120g, 4oz) dates, chopped

1½ cups (375ml, 13fl oz) soy milk

½ cup (125ml, 4fl oz) vegetable oil

1 large egg, beaten

1 cup (100g, 3½ oz) frozen blueberries

Preheat oven to 200°C (390°F, Gas Mark 6). Line a 12-hole muffin tin with paper cases.

Combine all ingredients in large bowl, stir until just combined. Transfer to the fridge and chill for 2 hours. Spoon the batter into the prepared paper cases so they are two-thirds full. Place in the oven and bake for 20 minutes.

The muffins are done when the tops looked cracked and golden brown and when a skewer inserted in the centre comes out clean. Remove from the oven, allow to stand for 5 minutes before cooling completely on a wire rack.

Raisin Compote

SERVES 6

4 apples, peeled, cored and chopped into 1cm (½ in) cubes

⅓ cup (115g, 4oz) maple syrup

1 tbsp lemon juice

2 cloves

¼ tsp allspice

2 tbsps brandy

½ cup (80g, 3oz) raisins

½ cup (80g, 3oz) sultanas

1 cup (190g, 7oz) dried apricots, halved

Place the apple pieces and lemon juice in a medium saucepan. Drizzle over the maple syrup.

Heat over medium heat for 5 minutes until the syrup begins to bubble. Reduce the heat to low, stir in the cloves and allspice and continue cooking for another 5 minutes.

Add the brandy, raisins, sultanas and apricots. Stir through, cover and cook for another 10 minutes.

Remove from heat and cool before serving.

SUGAR AND BERRIES

Here are the superstars of the delicious berry world: one cup of strawberries contains 7 grams of natural sugar and an entire day's worth of vitamin C. The same amount of raspberries contains 5 grams of sugar and 8 grams of fibre … and so much happiness. Add one more cup of sparkling, seedy blackberries — there's another 7 grams of sugar, along with 8 grams of fibre and 2 grams of protein. It sounds like a lot of sugar, but it's all natural (much better than the chocolate biscuit and the spoonful of sugar in coffee), plus there are all the other wonderful nutritional benefits of these lovely berries to balance the sugar, too.

Chocolate Berry Balls

BRIGHT, TASTY BOMBS OF FLAVOUR, THESE FUN CHOCOLATE BALLS ARE GREAT TREATS FOR THE KIDS

MAKES 16

2 cups (250g, 8oz) raw cashew nuts

1 cup (115g, 4oz) goji berries

1 vanilla bean, scraped, or 1 tsp of vanilla extract or paste

2 tbsps cacao powder

8 large medjool dates, pitted

½ cup (125g, 4oz) raspberries

1 cup (90g, 3oz) desiccated coconut

In a food processor or powerful blender, grind the cashew nuts to a fine meal.

Add the goji berries and vanilla and cacao and whizz until fine. This should turn the nut meal pink (pinkish, anyway!).

Add the dates, one at a time, and then transfer to a bowl before adding and mixing half the desiccated coconut.

Place the raspberries into a blender and blend until pureed. Pour the puree into a shallow bowl.

Lightly dip the balls into the raspberry puree, shaking off any excess, then roll in the rest of the coconut to coat.

Refrigerate before serving.

Strawberry Galette

SERVES 6

PASTRY

2 cups (240g, 8oz) almond meal

²/₃ cup (80g, 3oz) tapioca flour

125g (4oz) butter, cubed and chilled

2 tsps maple syrup

½ tsp salt

1 egg, lightly beaten

1 tsp apple cider vinegar

4 tbsps ice-cold water

FILLING

½ cup (50g, 2oz) almond meal

1 tbsp plain flour

¼ cup (90g, 3oz) maple syrup

1 tsp vanilla extract

700g (1½ lb) strawberries, hulled and halved

1 tsp lemon juice

Greek yoghurt, to serve

Preheat oven to 200°C (400°F, Gas Mark 6). Line a baking tray with baking paper.

To make the pastry, place the almond meal and flour into a blender with the butter. Pulse several times until it resembles breadcrumbs. Mix in the maple syrup, salt, egg, vinegar and half the water.

Pulse again until the mixture begins to comes together.

Using your hands, bring the dough together, adding more water as needed. Shape into a large disc, wrap it in plastic wrap and place in the fridge for at least 30 minutes.

To make the filling, mix together the almond meal, flour and maple syrup and set aside.

Roll out the dough into a circle about 5mm (¼ in) thick.

Spread the filling mixture over the pastry, leaving at least a 4cm (1½ in) margin all along the edge.

Heat the strawberries in a medium saucepan over medium heat until they have slightly softened. Let them cool for 15 minutes, then arrange them over the filling mixture.

Gently fold the edges of the dough up over the strawberries, crimping it down with your fingers.

Bake for 30 minutes until the crust is golden brown.

Serve warm with a dollop of fresh Greek yoghurt

Baked Apples with Honey and Walnuts

SPICY, SWEET AND COMFORTING, THESE BAKED APPLES ARE A
LOVELY CHOICE FOR DESSERT ON A COLD WINTER'S NIGHT

SERVES 6

6 baking apples

½ cup (80g, 3oz) sultanas

¼ cup (30g, 1oz) walnuts, chopped

¼ cup (30g, 1oz) hazelnuts, chopped

1 tbsp cinnamon

60g (2oz) butter

¼ cup (60ml, 2fl oz) apple juice

3 tbsps honey

Walnut halves, to garnish

Preheat oven to 200°C (400°F, Gas Mark 6) and grease a deep oven dish with a lid.

With a sharp knife, remove the top third of the apples and remove the core from each.

In a mixing bowl, mix together the sultanas, walnuts, hazelnuts and cinnamon. Fill the apple cavities with the nut mixture. Add a knob of butter onto each and replace the top third of the apple. Place the apples into the prepared dish and cover with the lid.

Place in the oven and bake for 30 minutes until apples are very soft.

Remove apples from oven and immediately transfer to a serving dish.

In a small saucepan, heat the apple juice, honey and any juices from the baking tray over medium-high heat until it begins to boil.

Immediately remove from the heat and spoon over the apples.

Serve with walnut halves and a dusting of icing sugar.

RAW HONEY

Bees are superstars of the planet and these genius golden creatures have been getting the glory they deserve — they are crucial for food production all over the world, as they drive the pollination process that allows plants to grow and produce, from almond to avocado trees. They also, of course, provide the world with honey. Sweet honeys, woody honeys, honeys that taste like vanilla or lavender or orange zest. Honey is an 'it' ingredient in healthy diets — it is an obvious, delicious substitute for sugar and highly processed sweet products. And while there are myriad brands, the spotlight is on organic honey as well as raw honey, both of which are less processed and have healing qualities for everything from seasonal allergies to skin conditions.

IT'S ALL IN THE HEAT

Organic honey is often extracted cold from the hives, then heated to remove impurities before being placed in a jar and sold. Cold extraction preserves some of the natural goodness, and heating then softens the honey and mellows out the flavours. The heating process also helps purify the honey. On the downside, heating reduces antioxidant and pollen content, which is where the medical magic is.

Raw honey is bursting with pollen It is never heated or purified — the sticky stuff has basically been scooped from the hives into the jar. Raw honey contains the natural antioxidants and enzymes that are lost in the processing of most supermarket brands. Eating raw honey has what's called a 'pre-biotic' effect — it soothes the gut with healthy bacteria, helping keep digestive systems balanced. Manuka honey is the most sophisticated strain of raw honey, sometimes prescribed by doctors and nutritionists as a natural antibiotic. Manuka honey can also be used to treat burns and it can prevent and heal skin infections.

DON'T OVERDOSE

While organic and raw honey are less processed, they both contain natural fructose, which should be eaten in moderation. Honey is better than sugar for weight loss, but it's not to be eaten by the jarful.

BEE POLLEN, ANYONE?

In juice shops and cafes, it's not just tea with honey anymore. Pollen is the byproduct of honey — the bees pack pollen in the hives for the queen bee to use and this is also extracted and bottled. The golden grains of pollen contain carbohydrates, protein, fat, vitamins, minerals and antioxidants. Pollen can be scooped into a fresh juice or nut milk smoothie.

Citrus and Honey Ice Cream

SERVES 4

2 oranges, peeled, seeds removed, and chopped

1½ cups (260g, 9oz) dates, pitted and chopped

½ cup (180g, 6oz) honey

½ cup (125ml, 4fl oz) coconut cream

Pinch of salt

2 tbsps coconut oil

Add the oranges to a food processor and pulse a few times.

Add the dates, honey, coconut cream, salt and oil.

Blend until smooth.

Pour into a large bowl, cover with plastic wrap and place in the freezer for 1 hour.

Remove from the freezer and blend again until smooth.

Place into an airtight container and freeze for at least 4 hours, preferably overnight.

Serve chilled.

Berry and Yoghurt Popsicles

A FRESH, HEALTHY SUMMER TREAT THAT'S FULL OF
GOODNESS AND LOOKS OH-SO PRETTY

MAKES 6

1 cup (250g, 9oz) Greek
yoghurt

½ cup (125ml, 4fl oz)
water

1 tsp vanilla extract

2 tbsps honey

1 cup (100g, 3½ oz)
blueberries

1 cup (125g, 4oz) fresh
raspberries

¼ cup (30g, 1oz)
pistachios, roughly
chopped

Mix yoghurt, water, vanilla and honey in a large bowl.

Have ready 6 plastic cups. Fill half of each cup with the yoghurt
mix.

Place the berries in a blender and blend until smooth.

Fill cups to the top with the berry mix, and insert popsicle sticks.

Sprinkle 1 teaspoon of pistachios over the top of each berry mix.

Transfer to the freezer and freeze for 8 hours.

Pink Grapefruit Sorbet

A BRIGHT AND REFRESHING SUMMER DESSERT THAT'S EASY TO MAKE AND ENJOY

SERVES 6

2 cups (500ml, 1pt) freshly squeezed pink grapefruit juice

1 cup (350g, 12oz) agave syrup

1¼ cups (310ml, 10fl oz) water

1 tsp grapefruit zest

2 tbsps freshly squeezed lemon juice

3 tbsps coconut cream

Mint sprigs, to garnish

Bring the grapefruit juice, agave syrup and water to boil in a medium saucepan, stirring continuously.

Once it boils, reduce the heat to low and add the zest and lemon juice. Stir to combine and let cool for 15 minutes.

Using a fine-mesh sieve, sieve the mixture into an airtight container and place in the fridge for 4 hours.

Place the mixture into a blender and blend until smooth.

Return to the container and refrigerate overnight.

Scoop the sorbet into the blender, add the coconut cream and puree again until smooth.

Place into an airtight container and freeze for at least 1 hour before serving.

Garnish with mint sprigs.

Rhubarb and White Chocolate Tart

THIS DECADENT DESSERT IS SURE TO IMPRESS, AND YOUR GUESTS MAY BE SURPRISED WHEN YOU TELL THEM THE INGREDIENTS

SERVES 8

PASTRY

1 tbsp ground flaxseeds

2 tbsps water

1⅓ cups (180g, 6oz) almond meal

2 tbsps maple syrup

⅓ cup (60g, 2oz) apple sauce

FILLING

½ cup (110g, 4oz) raw sugar

¼ cup (30g, 1oz) custard powder

1¼ cups (310ml, 10fl oz) almond milk

½ tsp vanilla extract

250g (9oz) silken tofu

125g (4oz) white baking chocolate, melted and cooled slightly

300g (10oz) rhubarb, cut into 6cm (2½ in) lengths

Zest of 1 orange and juice of ½ orange

¼ cup (90g, 3oz) maple syrup, extra

Mix together the ground flaxseed with the water and set aside. Blend together the almond meal, maple syrup and apple sauce in a food processor until it looks like breadcrumbs. Add the flaxseed mixture and process briefly until mixture begins to come together.

Remove from the food processer and gently knead together for 1 minute. Form it into a large disc. Wrap in plastic wrap and refrigerate for at least 30 minutes.

Preheat oven to 200°C (400°F, Gas Mark 6) and line a 35 x 12cm (14 x 5in) rectangular fluted tart pan with baking paper.

Roll the pastry out to form a large rectangle and place in the tart pan, ensuring it comes up to the top of the sides.

Prick the base with a fork, line with foil and fill with baking beads or rice.Bake for 15 minutes, reduce the heat to 180°C (350°F, Gas Mark 4) and bake for 10 more minutes until the edges are browned.

To make the filling, heat the raw sugar and custard powder in a saucepan over medium heat until boiling. When the mix starts to thicken, gradually whisk in the almond milk and vanilla extract. Remove from the heat, place in an airtight container and place in the fridge for 30 minutes until cold.

Place in a blender and puree with the silken tofu until smooth. Return to the container and chill in the fridge until the mixture has firmed up.

Mix through the melted white chocolate and chill again.

In a medium saucepan, gently heat the rhubarb, orange zest, orange juice and extra maple syrup over medium heat until it begins to bubble. Reduce the heat to low and cook for 10 minutes.

To assemble the tart, spread the chocolate mixture evenly over the base and arrange the rhubarb over the top, then serve.

Rhubarb Jam

MAKES 500ML

500g (1lb 2oz) trimmed rhubarb, washed, roughly chopped

2 cups (500g, 1lb 2oz) raw sugar

1 tsp fresh ginger, minced

2 tbsps lemon juice

1 tsp vanilla extract

Combine the rhubarb, sugar, ginger, lemon juice and vanilla in a large bowl. Cover and leave overnight

Heat the mixture in a large saucepan over medium-high heat.

Bring the mixture to a boil. If you get any froth forming on the top, use a large flat spoon to skim it off and dispose.

Cook for 30 minutes, until the jam has thickened. Smear a little over a chilled spoon and if it thickens to a jam consistency, then it's ready.

Place the jam in a clean, dry 500ml-capacity jar or two 250ml jars and seal.

Jam will keep for up to 2 months.

Red Cordial

MAKES 4 CUPS

300g (10oz) ripe strawberries, hulled and roughly chopped

180g (6oz) rhubarb, chopped into 2cm (1in) pieces

3 limes, juiced

¾ cup (260g, 9oz) maple syrup

4 cups (1L, 2pt) water

Basil sprigs, to garnish

Add all the ingredients to a large saucepan and bring to a boil. Reduce the heat to low and simmer for 10 minutes until the fruit has begun to soften. Stir to break up the rhubarb and strawberries. Gently simmer, covered, for a further 20 minutes.

Remove from the heat and let the mixture cool to room temperature.

Strain the liquid into a jug or glass bottle through a fine sieve or piece of muslin.

Press down on the fruit while straining to ensure all the juice is pushed through.

Serve, diluted to taste with still or sparkling water.

Garnish with basil leaves.

RHUBARB

Rhubarb is actually a vegetable — it grows tall and wild in long green and deep-red fronds and is bursting with natural fibre, calcium, potassium and vitamin K. It's lovely to eat when stewed up and spooned over cereal in the morning or yoghurt for dessert. The challenge is: sweetness. Rhubarb is naturally bitter, which makes it an excellent complement to sweet dishes like cheesecake or ice cream. Otherwise, stew it with some raw honey and berries, then pour them all into an almond-meal pie crust for a gorgeous crumble. Yum.

Strawberry and Redcurrant Polenta Cake

A FILLING AFTERNOON TREAT THAT CAN BE ENJOYED WITHOUT ANY NASTY SUGAR RUSH

SERVES 12

4 tbsps ground flaxseeds

½ cup (120ml, 4fl oz) water

1⅓ cups (210g, 8oz) polenta

⅔ cup (80g, 3oz) plain flour

½ tsp salt

1 tsp baking powder

½ cup (80g, 3oz) apple sauce

1¼ cups (275g, 10oz) raw sugar

1 tsp vanilla extract

½ cup (125g, 4oz) Greek yoghurt

1 cup (200g, 7oz) fresh strawberries, sliced, plus 2 whole strawberries for garnish

½ cup (50g, 2oz) redcurrants (fresh or frozen), plus 2 tbsps for garnish

¼ cup (30g, 1oz) flaked almonds

Preheat oven to 180°C (350°F, Gas Mark 4). Grease and lightly dust with flour a 23 x 4cm (9 x 1.5in) round cake tin.

Mix the ground flaxseed together with the water and set aside.

Sift together the polenta, flour, salt and baking powder and set aside.

In a food processor, blend together the apple sauce and sugar until thoroughly combined. Mix in the flaxseed mixture and vanilla extract and thoroughly combine.

Add the polenta mixture and the yoghurt, a third at a time, combining thoroughly before adding the next portion.

Gently fold in the strawberries and redcurrants.

Pour the batter into the cake tin and sprinkle over the almond flakes.

Bake for 45 to 50 minutes in the oven or until a skewer inserted into the middle comes out clean.

Let the cake cool for 20 minutes before turning out onto a wire rack.

Halve the strawberries and place in the centre of the cake and sprinkle over the extra redcurrants.

SAVOURY SWEET

Ever thought of grating carrots into a bowl of rice for dessert? This could be the start of a delicious and healthy rice pudding. Cook with a nut milk or coconut milk, grated carrots, some vanilla, raisins and cardamom and there's a sweet treat to snack on for days. Vegetables are not only for dinner: carrot, zucchini, pumpkin, sweet potato and even parsnip can be the starter, main course, dessert or a treat.

SWEET POTATO

Sweet potato works wonders for special occasions. Try using mashed sweet potato to make fudgy, moist chocolate brownies. Substitute maple syrup for sugar, and cocoa or cacao powder rather than chocolate. The resulting muffins are dense and indulgent, rather than light and fluffy.

BEETROOT

Beetroots, those gorgeous deep-red and purple vegetables, are bursting with natural sugar. They can be juiced or grated into baked goods and creamy desserts without interfering with blood sugar levels. Beetroot is a winner in chocolate cake. It is the red in the classic American 'red velvet cake', which is simply a chocolate cake made with the juice of beetroots. This cake can even be made without chocolate — cacao powder is just as rich as cocoa and chocolate, and without the sugar. To make it even healthier you can use almond meal instead of flour, olive or coconut oil instead of butter, and frozen raspberries for extra natural sugar.

CARAMELISED ONION

Caramelised onions with fresh tomatoes on burgers are a perfect substitute for sugary, bottled ketchup. Soft and rich, they're also excellent in tarts — mix them with goat's cheese and spoon into puff pastry cases for an appetizer or dessert. Slowly caramelise onions in oil or butter on low heat.

ZUCCHINI

Mid-morning muffins don't need to be naughty. Zucchini blends beautifully with coconut for a cupcake, muffin or brownie. The vegetable adds moistness to baked goods, as well as vital nutrients, and provides an amazing way to sneak veggies into the kids' lunchboxes.

For pie crumbs and tart bases, consider grinding almonds with a zucchini to create a crunchy, crumbly base. Carrots or parsnips can also be used — the nuts and vegetables balance savoury and sweet flavours, giving a slight earthy, salty tang.

Pumpkin Oat Scones

AFTERNOON TEA WILL BE A REFUELLING AFFAIR THANKS TO
THESE HIGH-ENERGY SCONES SWEETENED WITH PUMPKIN

SERVES 8

2 cups (250g, 8oz) plain
flour

1 cup (90g, 3oz) rolled
oats, reserve 2 tbsps

¹/₃ cup (70g, 2½ oz)
raw sugar

1 tbsp baking powder

¾ tsp salt

¾ tsp cinnamon

½ tsp nutmeg

½ tsp allspice

125g (4oz) butter,
chilled and cubed

²/₃ cup (150g, 5oz)
pumpkin, mashed

2 eggs

Line a baking tray with baking paper.

In a large mixing bowl, combine flour, oats, sugar, baking
powder, salt and spices. Add butter to the dry ingredients,
rubbing with fingertips to create a coarse crumb.

In a separate bowl, beat the mashed pumpkin and eggs together
well. Add wet ingredients to the dry ingredients and bring the
dough together with your hands.

Place dough onto a sheet of greaseproof paper and flatten using
your hands or a rolling pin until 3cm (1in) thick. Cut into eight
triangles and lay the individual scones on the lined tray.

Transfer to the freezer for 30 minutes.

Preheat oven to 220°C (430°F, Gas Mark 7) 10 minutes before
scones are due out of the freezer.

Remove from the freezer and sprinkle the reserved oats over the
top of the scones.

Place in oven and bake for 20 to 25 minutes, until a skewer
inserted into the centre comes out clean.

Remove from oven and allow to stand for 5 minutes before
cooling completely on a wire rack.

Caramelised Red Onion Tartlets

THESE BITE-SIZED BURSTS OF FLAVOUR MAKE AN AMAZING DELICIOUS CHANGE FROM THE USUAL DESSERT OPTIONS

MAKES 8

4 red onions, peeled and halved, ends trimmed

3 tbsps olive oil

3 tbsps brown sugar

Salt and freshly ground black pepper

1 cup (250ml, 8fl oz) red wine

2 sheets puff pastry

2 tbsps milk

Sprigs of thyme, to garnish

Preheat oven to 190°C (375°F, Gas Mark 5).

Place the onions snugly into a small baking dish with high sides, cut side up. Drizzle over the olive oil and sprinkle over the brown sugar and salt and pepper. Pour half a tablespoon of red wine over each half.

Bake in the oven for 30 minutes. Take out and pour another half-tablespoon of wine over each half and return to the oven for another 15 minutes or until they have caramelised and are cooked through.

Reduce the oven to 180°C (350°F, Gas Mark 4).

Cut the pastry into 8cm (3in) diameter circles (or so that they're slightly larger than the onion halves by 1cm or ½ in).

Score a shallow rim 1cm from the edge of the pastry circles. Brush the edges of the circles with milk.

Bake the cases in the oven for 10 minutes.

Gently push down on the inner circles of each case to create a shallow depression.

Place each onion into the centre of each tart and serve garnished with thyme.

Pumpkin Bread

SERVES 8

2 tbsps ground flaxseeds

4 tbsps water

2 cups (250g, 8oz) plain flour

1 tsp bicarbonate of soda

½ tsp salt

1 tsp ground cinnamon

¼ tsp ground ginger

1½ cups (340g, 12oz) butternut pumpkin, mashed

½ cup (125ml, 4fl oz) vegetable oil

½ cup (180g, 6oz) maple syrup

¼ cup (40g, 1½ oz) brown sugar

3 tbsps pepitas (pumpkin seeds)

Preheat oven to 180°C (350°F, Gas Mark 4). Grease and flour a loaf tin. Mix together flaxseed and water in a bowl and sit for 15 minutes. In a large bowl, mix flour, bicarb, salt, cinnamon and ginger. Make a well in the centre. In another bowl, combine flaxseed mixture, pumpkin, oil, maple syrup and brown sugar. Stir the wet ingredients into the dry ingredients until just blended. Pour into loaf tin and sprinkle the pepitas over top. Bake for 50 minutes until a skewer inserted into the middle comes out clean. Rest for 10 minutes before turning out onto a wire rack.

20-Minute Pumpkin Butter

MAKES 4–5 CUPS

2 cups (425g, 15oz) butternut pumpkin, cooked and pureed

²⁄₃ cup (140g, 5oz) raw sugar

¼ cup (90g, 3oz) maple syrup

½ cup (125ml, 4fl oz) pear juice

1 tbsp lemon juice

½ tsp cinnamon

¼ tsp ground cloves

¼ tsp allspice

Pinch of sea salt

Mix together all the ingredients in a medium saucepan and heat over medium-high heat until beginning to boil.

Reduce heat to low and simmer for 20 minutes (you can cook for longer!).

Taste and adjust with any of the ingredients to make it more to your taste.

Once cooled completely, transfer to a couple of clean, dry glass jars and seal.

It will keep in the fridge for up to 2 weeks.

MAPLE SYRUP

Maple syrup is the byproduct of boiling down the sap of the sugar maple tree that grows in Eastern Canada and Northern USA. Sounds romantic, huh? And we all know it's delicious. It's less intensively processed than white sugar, and has health benefits too: high quantities of the minerals manganese, potassium, calcium and zinc. But if it's a low sugar diet you are after, be wary of this sweet nectar. It does contain sugar and the darker the syrup, the more sugar it contains. Maple syrup is great for a treat.

Pumpkin Fruit Cookies

A GREAT AFTERNOON PICK-ME-UP THAT'S PACKED FULL OF ENERGIZING INGREDIENTS FOR EVERYONE TO ENJOY

MAKES 30

200g (7oz) butter, softened

½ cup (110g, 4oz) raw sugar

1 cup (225g, 8oz) pumpkin, mashed

1 egg

1 tsp vanilla extract

2 cups (250g, 8oz) whole-wheat or plain flour

1 cup (90g, 3oz) oats

¾ cup (120g, 4oz) dried cranberries

¹/₃ cup (45g, 1½ oz) pepitas (pumpkin seeds)

1 tsp ground cinnamon

1 tsp bicarbonate of soda

½ tsp baking powder

1 tsp salt

Preheat oven to 190°C (375°F, Gas Mark 5).

Using a hand-held electric mixer, beat butter and sugar until creamy and combined.

Add pumpkin, egg and vanilla and beat until smooth.

Place flour, oats, cranberries, pepitas, cinnamon, bicarb, baking powder and salt in a separate bowl and stir to combine.

Fold creamed butter and pumpkin into dry ingredients.

Spoon 2 tablespoons of batter per cookie onto a lined baking tray. Flatten slightly and shape into rounds.

Place in the oven and bake for 15 minutes, until golden.

Remove from the oven and place on a wire rack to cool.

Paleo

BASIC PRINCIPLES OF PALEO

'Going Paleo' is a little like taking a trip back to the time of cavemen and women. For them, eating was about energy and comfort — meat was eaten fat and all, which provided warmth and fuel. Vegetables and fruits were picked as they grew in the season. For us today, it might mean eating the way a great-grandmother ate before frozen foods and instant snacks packed the aisles of supermarkets. The Paleo diet is all about eating real food and cutting out preservatives and additives.

PALEO FOOD: IN

- unprocessed meats
- fish
- eggs
- vegetables
- fruits
- nuts

PALEO FOOD: OUT

- foods that are processed, packaged and frozen
- cereal or grains like wheat, corn and rice
- legumes, including beans and peanuts
- dairy products
- sugar and corn syrup
- artificial colouring, flavouring and preservatives

WHY GO PALEO?

Although the jury is out on the medical benefits of the Paleo diet, anecdotally at least it has helped people heal digestive and allergy issues that have long baffled doctors. It is said to help prevent some of the most common chronic diseases. Weight loss can be a natural side effect of the diet too. Critics say that the elimination of basic food groups, including dairy, grains, rice and legumes, makes it challenging to get all essential nutrients for a healthy body.

Going Paleo is a big transition and it is possible to gain many of the upsides of the diet without following the guidelines strictly and immediately.

TIPS FOR GOING PALEO

- Eggs are amazing. Look for omega-3-enriched, cage-free eggs.
- Olive, coconut and avocado oil are favoured cooking oils.
- Nuts are high in calories so great for a snack, but resist eating bags and bags of them.
- Sweet potatoes are excellent energy food as well a sugar substitute.
- Have treats: allow a day or even a week to indulge.
- Move: exercise is crucial for any diet and lifestyle.

Beef and Golden Beetroot Stew

THIS PERFECTLY SLOW-COOKED MEAL IS WHAT WINTER
WEEKENDS WERE MADE FOR

SERVES 6

4 tbsps olive oil

650g (1lb 7oz) stewing beef (chuck or beef cheek) cut into 3cm (1in) chunks

1 large onion, finely diced

4 cloves garlic, minced

2 large golden beetroots, peeled, cut into 1.5cm (½ in) cubes

4 stalks celery, chopped

1 cup (250ml, 8fl oz) red wine

4 cups (1L, 2pt) beef stock

1 x 400g (14oz) can chopped tomatoes

1 tsp dried thyme

¼ cup (10g, ¼ oz) fresh parsley, chopped

Zest of ½ orange

1 tbsp orange zest strands, to garnish

Sea salt and pepper, to taste

Heat half the olive oil in a large pot over medium-high heat. Add the beef in batches, cooking for 3 minutes until browned all over. Remove from the pot and set aside. Add the rest of the oil and add the onion and garlic and saute for 5 minutes, until the onion is translucent.

Add the beetroot and celery and saute for 3 minutes.

Return the beef to the pot along with the wine and bring to a boil.

Add the stock, chopped tomatoes, thyme, half the parsley and the orange zest to the pot.

Bring to the boil, then reduce the heat and gently simmer, covered, for at least 2 hours (the longer this cooks, the more tender the meat will become).

Season with salt and pepper and serve with a couple of parsley leaves and strands of orange zest to garnish.

Lamb Broth with Grilled Chops

A LITTLE TIME IS REQUIRED TO DELIVER THE FLAVOUR THIS BROTH IS CAPABLE OF PRODUCING. IT'S TIME WELL SPENT

SERVES 4

BROTH

500g (1lb) lamb bones

2 tbsps olive oil

1 onion, chopped

6 cloves garlic, peeled and halved

1/3 cup (80ml, 3fl oz) dry white wine

3 tomatoes, chopped

2 carrots, sliced

1 stalk celery, sliced

½ small fennel bulb, chopped

1 tsp black peppercorns

2 bay leaves

A few stalks of oregano and flat-leaf parsley, tied together

CHOPS

4 cloves garlic, crushed

2 tsps ground cumin

2 tbsps chilli flakes

½ tsp salt

½ tsp freshly ground pepper

2 tbsps olive oil

8 lamb chops

Preheat oven to 220°C (425°F, Gas Mark 7).

Lay the lamb bones out in a large roasting tray and splash over a couple of slugs of olive oil. Roast the bones for 20 minutes, then turn over and roast for a further 20 minutes.

Heat the oil in a large stockpot over medium-high heat. Add the onion and garlic and saute for 5 minutes, until the onion is translucent.

Pour in the wine and bring to a boil and add the rest of the stock ingredients.

Place the roasted lamb bones in the pot and add enough water to sit above the bones by about 2cm (1in). Bring to the boil, then reduce the heat to low and simmer for at least 3 hours. Use a flat spoon to skim off any froth that gathers on the top.

Once you're happy with the stock flavour, turn off the heat and let it cool for 20 minutes. Strain the stock liquid through a fine mesh sieve and discard the stock ingredients.

Cool the stock in the fridge for at least 3 hours. Remove any fat that has congealed on the surface.

To prepare the lamb, in a small bowl mix together the garlic, cumin, half the chilli flakes, salt and pepper and the olive oil. Rub this into the lamb chops and let them sit for at least 30 minutes in the fridge.

Heat a grill plate over high heat. Cook the lamb chops for 3 minutes on each side. Let them sit for 3 minutes before serving.

Serve chops in a small bowl of hot stock with a sprinkling of chilli flakes for garnish.

Slow-Cooked Pork with Apple Sauce

SLOW-COOKED PORK AND APPLE SAUCE IS A CLASSIC FLAVOUR
COMBINATION THAT MAKES FOR A LOVELY WINTER DINNER

SERVES 8

1 onion, thinly sliced

4 cloves garlic, crushed

2 cups (500ml, 1pt) chicken stock

3 tbsps Cajun seasoning

1 tbsp dark brown sugar

1 x 2kg (5lb) pork shoulder, boneless or bone-in

⅓ cup (15g, ½ oz) fresh parsley, chopped

800g (1¾ lb) fresh green beans, ends trimmed, cut into 3cm (1in) sections

APPLE SAUCE

10 red apples, peeled, cored and sliced

2 large lemons, juiced

4 tbsps brown sugar

Preheat the oven to 135°C (275°F, Gas Mark 1).

Spread the onions and garlic in a large roasting tray and pour over the chicken stock.

Combine the Cajun seasoning and brown sugar in a small bowl.

Pat the pork shoulder dry with kitchen paper and score with a sharp knife. Rub vigorously with spice mixture.

Place the pork on top of the onion and garlic and cover with foil.

Transfer to the oven and cook for 6 to 8 hours, until the pork is fork tender.

While the pork is cooking, make the apple sauce. With just enough water to cover the apples, bring apples, lemon juice and sugar to the boil over a high heat. Reduce heat and simmer for 30 minutes until apples fall apart. Drain excess water and mash apples until smooth.

Remove the pork to a cutting board and shred into bite-sized pieces.

Boil the beans in a large pot of lightly salted water for 4 minutes.

Serve the pork with the beans on the side and with a couple of spoonfuls of the sauce over the top. Sprinkle pork with parsley for garnish.

Roasted Chicken with Lemon, Garlic and Olives

BOLD FLAVOURS ELEVATE THIS FRESH MEDITERRANEAN TAKE ON THE TRADITIONAL ROAST

SERVES 4

1kg (2lb) chicken pieces (drumsticks, breasts, thighs)

2 lemons, zested and then cut into quarters

3 tbsps salt flakes

1½ tbsps chilli flakes

2 tbsps soy sauce

6 sprigs rosemary, chop the leaves from 2 sprigs

⅓ cup (70ml, 2½ fl oz) olive oil

1 bulb garlic, sliced in half crosswise

1 cup (180g, 6oz) kalamata olives, whole or pitted

Preheat oven to 230°C (450°F, Gas Mark 8). Heat a large roasting dish in the oven.

Pat dry the chicken pieces and place in a large bowl.

Squeeze a lemon quarter over the chicken pieces and then add the lemon zest, salt flakes, chilli flakes, soy sauce, chopped rosemary and half the olive oil to the bowl. Toss the pieces to coat them thoroughly and rub as much of the mix as you can into the pieces.

Place the chicken pieces into the hot roasting dish, skin side down, along with the two garlic halves, cut sides down. Drizzle over any remaining oil from the bowl, as well as the rest of the olive oil, the rest of the lemon quarters and 2 rosemary sprigs.

Bake in the oven for 30 minutes, then remove and turn the pieces and garlic halves over

Reduce the oven to 200°C (400°F, Gas Mark 6) and add the olives to the dish.

Cook for a further 30 minutes until the chicken skin is golden brown.

Remove the dish from the oven and let sit for 5 minutes before serving.

Serve garnished with rosemary leaves.

Pork Belly with Shoestring Onions and Chinese Broccoli

AN ASIAN CLASSIC THAT COMBINES CRISPY, SALTY AND SWEET
FLAVOURS WITH MELTINGLY TENDER MEAT

SERVES 4

PORK

700g (1½ lb) pork belly, skin on

MARINADE

1 tsp salt

1 egg, lightly beaten

¼ tsp five-spice powder

1 tbsp brown sugar

½ tbsp chilli powder

1 tbsp Chinese rice wine

ONIONS

Canola oil, for frying

4 tsps cornflour

1 tsp salt

Freshly ground black pepper

2 medium onions, quartered and cut into thin slices

CHINESE BROCCOLI

2 bunches Chinese broccoli, ends trimmed

¼ cup (60ml, 2fl oz) soy sauce

2 cloves garlic, minced

1 tbsps fresh ginger, minced

1 tbsp balsamic vinegar

1 tsp sesame oil

Mix together all the pork marinade ingredients in a small bowl then pour over the pork belly and marinate overnight in the fridge. Marinate pork belly with all ingredients except the flours, for at least 3 hours or overnight in the fridge.

Preheat the oven to 180°C (350°F, Gas Mark 4). Place the pork belly on a wire rack over a roasting tray and cook for 1 hour. Remove from the oven and rest for 20 minutes before slicing.

Meanwhile to make the onions, pour oil in a deep pot to 1.5cm (½ in) deep. Heat the oil to 170°C (340°F).

Mix the cornflour with the salt and a couple of grinds of pepper. Pat dry the onions then lightly coat them in the flour.

Fry the onions in the hot oil in small batches for about 12 minutes until they're dark golden brown. Remove from the pot with a slotted spoon and drain on paper towels.

Boil the Chinese broccoli in lightly salted water for 5 minutes until tender and the leaves are wilted.

Mix together the soy sauce, garlic, ginger, vinegar and sesame oil in a small bowl.

To serve, pour the soy dressing over the cooked broccoli, place the hot pork belly slices on the broccoli. Garnish with the crispy fried onions.

Pickled Mushrooms

SERVES 4

225g (8oz, ½ lb) button mushrooms

3 tbsps olive oil

2 tbsps lemon juice

2 tsps light soy sauce

1 tbsp apple cider vinegar

1 tbsp maple syrup

2 bay leaves

¼ cup (10g, ¼ oz) dill, chopped

4 cloves garlic, thinly sliced

Wash and dry mushrooms. Place in a glass jar or plastic container.

Mix together the oil, lemon juice, soy sauce, vinegar, maple syrup, bay leaves, dill and garlic.

Pour the marinade over the mushrooms and toss to fully coat.

Refrigerate for 4 hours, stirring every hour.

Sauteed Mushrooms

SERVES 4

400g (14oz) shitake mushrooms, halved

2 tbsps olive oil

3 cloves garlic, minced

3 spring onions, sliced

200g (7oz) cherry tomatoes

3 tbsps tamari (or soy sauce)

3 tbsps balsamic vinegar

2 tsps salt

Freshly ground black pepper

1 tbsp fresh parsley, chopped

Heat the olive in a large frying pan over medium heat. Add the garlic and saute for 2 minutes.

Add the mushrooms and saute for a further 4 minutes.

Add the spring onions and tomatoes to the pan and cook for 5 minutes, stirring occasionally.

Add the tamari, vinegar, salt and a couple of grinds of pepper.

Cover and let it cook for 10 minutes. Mix through the parsley and serve hot.

SHITAKE
MUSHROOMS

Gorgeous, velvety shitake mushrooms have a lightly meaty,
distinctly savoury flavour and are packed full of nutrients
and antioxidants that the cavepeople could thrive on.
They are also high in vitamin D, so great for long winters.
Thrown whole into a stew of red meat or pork and lots of
vegetables, they add satisfying peppery bites and also lend
a creaminess, which blends beautifully with a cream base
or as a substitute if going dairy-free. Shitake mushrooms
are big in Chinese cuisine, which includes them in stir-fries
with eggplant as well as spicy, hearty soup broths.

OFFAL

Said in some accents, it sounds like 'awful'. And perhaps some might agree, because offal refers to the innards of an animal. Offal is the original survival food, packed full of energy, protein and nutrients that cavepeople and hard-working folk historically thrived on.

Organs, including kidneys, liver, brains and even tongue, plus blood, ears and feet, are turned into edible delicacies by chefs in fine-dining restaurants. Home chefs cook with offal too and it is consistent with a Paleo-style approach, embracing the concept of eating from the land and making the most of what nature provides, without waste.

SWEETBREADS: These are sweet but not in a doughnut sort of way. The pancreas or thymus of a veal or a lamb may be soaked in salt water, then poached in milk to soften and sweeten the organ. They are easiest to eat when pan-fried. Sweetbreads taste like light, fried meat and they are much healthier than fatty fried chicken. Sweetbreads are high sources of vitamin C and protein.

BRAINS: Brains are finer and gentler than other organs and are eaten for their soft, creamy texture. They may be poached like eggs and chopped into fine pieces, like chunky mince. They are popular scrambled with eggs for breakfast or pan-fried with vegetables for dinner.

BLOOD: Not as gory as it sounds, blood is usually served in a sausage. Black pudding is a traditional side served with egg, beans and mushrooms in an English breakfast. It is salty, a bit chewy, and tastes a bit like fried rice. In other parts of Europe, blood sausage is everywhere. It tastes like minced pork sausage: meaty and seasoned just with salt and pepper or bright herbs such as parsley or basil. Blood is a great source of iron.

OX CHEEK: Ox cheek has a strong, peppery flavour. It cooks up into soft, silky strands and is great for soup broths or vibrant sauces. It can be stewed with lots of vegetables or baked into a pie topped with mashed sweet potato.

LIVER: Pate and foie gras (meaning 'fat liver') are served in award-winning restaurants, sold in the party-foods sections of supermarkets, and easy enough to make at home. Calf and chicken livers are the most popular and beloved for their creamy texture. Some foie gras is made with the liver of a duck or goose — spread it on a salty rice cracker, or serve it up on an appetizer platter with pickled vegetables that blend beautifully with the buttery pate. Pate is often peppery or herby, as liver is mixed in with pungent flavours such as onion or chives.

Fried Liver with Onions

HERE'S A GOOD, WHOLESOME AND STRAIGHTFORWARD
INTRODUCTION TO COOKING WITH LIVER

SERVES 4

600g (1lb 5oz) beef liver

1 cup (125g, 4oz) flour

1 tsp chilli powder

1 tbsp fresh sage
leaves, finely chopped

1 tsp salt

Freshly ground pepper

2 tbsps coconut oil

2 medium onions, sliced

½ cup (125ml, 4fl oz)
vegetable oil

¼ cup (10g, ¼ oz)
chives, chopped

Rinse and pat dry the liver pieces.

Mix together the flour, chilli powder, sage leaves, salt and a
couple of good grinds of pepper and place in a shallow dish.

Heat the coconut oil in a large frying pan over medium heat.

Add the onion and saute for 20 minutes, until the onion has
softened and started to caramelise. Remove the onions from the
pan. Set aside and keep warm.

Coat the liver pieces in the flour mix.

Add the vegetable oil to the pan and heat it over medium-high
heat.

Fry the liver pieces for 3 minutes either side until cooked
through, but don't overcook or they'll become too tough.

Serve hot with the onions and a sprinkling of chives for garnish.

Chicken Liver Pate

THIS IS SO TASTY AND SO SIMPLE. YOU'LL WONDER WHY
YOU EVER BOUGHT IT AT THE SUPERMARKET

MAKES 2 JARS

300g (10oz) fresh
chicken livers

250g (9oz) unsalted
butter

¼ cup (25g, 1oz)
shallots, finely chopped

2 cloves garlic, minced

2 tbsps fresh thyme

3 tbsps cognac

Pinch of nutmeg

1 tsp freshly ground
black pepper

1 tsp salt flakes

4 sage leaves, to
garnish

⅓ cup (75ml, 2½ fl oz)
melted clarified butter

Rinse and pat dry the livers.

Heat 2 tablespoons of unsalted butter in a medium frying pan
over medium-high heat. Add the shallots and garlic and saute for
5 minutes.

Add the livers and thyme and fry for 4 minutes, flipping the
livers over halfway through.

Place the mix into a food processor and set aside.

Pour the cognac into the pan and scrape the bottom of the pan
to remove anything sticking to it. Pour the liquid into the food
processor.

Add the nutmeg, pepper, the rest of the unsalted butter, and a
pinch of salt flakes to the food processor.

Blend until the mixture is a smooth paste. Let it cool for 30
minutes.

Divide the pate in half and place in 2 x 250ml-capacity jars.

Place 2 leaves of sage on top.

Pour an even amount of the melted clarified butter into the top
of each jar.

Seal and store in the fridge.

Roasted Cauliflower with Lemon and Tahini Sauce

CAULIFLOWER WITH A MIDDLE EASTERN TWIST IS A LOVELY SIDE DISH THAT DOESN'T NEED MUCH ELSE TO MAKE A MEAL OF IT

SERVES 6

1 large head cauliflower, washed and broken into florets

1 tbsp coconut oil

1 small onion, quartered and sliced

2 tsps caraway seeds

½ cup (115g, 4oz) tahini

¼ cup (60ml, 2fl oz) lemon juice

½ cup (125ml, 4fl oz) warm water

2 cloves garlic, minced

¾ tsp salt

½ tsp cayenne pepper

¼ cup (10g, ¼ oz) fresh parsley leaves, chopped

Preheat oven to 220°C (425°F, Gas Mark 7).

Heat the oil in a large frying pan over medium-high heat.

Add the onion and saute for 5 minutes, until the onion has softened.

Place the onion in a large bowl with the cauliflower florets and caraway seeds.

In a bowl, whisk together the tahini, lemon juice, water, garlic, salt and cayenne pepper.

Spoon one-third of a cup of the sauce over the cauliflower and onions and toss to combine.

Place the cauliflower in a baking dish that has a lid and bake, covered, for 15 minutes.

Remove the lid, mix up the cauliflower and bake for a further 15 minutes or until the cauliflower is browned and tender.

Serve the cauliflower with the remaining tahini sauce on the side and the parsley sprinkled over for garnish.

Liver Baked with Mushrooms and Bacon

PACKED FULL OF NUTRIENTS, LIVER HELPS YOUR BODY PERFORM ITS OWN DETOX PROGRAM

SERVES 4

550g (1¼ lb) calf or beef livers

40g (1½ oz) unsalted butter

4 shallots, peeled and halved lengthways

2 cloves garlic, minced

4 rashers bacon, fat removed, cut into 3cm-thick (1in) slices

200g (7oz) of mushrooms, thickly sliced

2 carrots, cut into thick strips

2 tbsps fresh sage leaves, chopped

Dash of flaxseed oil

1 tsp Dijon mustard

2 tbsps cognac

2 tbsps light cream

Salt and pepper

¼ cup (10g, ¼ oz) fresh parsley leaves, finely chopped

Rinse and pat dry the liver and cut into 3cm-thick (1in) sections.

Heat the butter in a large frying pan over medium heat. Add the shallots and garlic and saute for 8 minutes, until the shallots are browned on the outside.

Add the bacon, mushrooms, carrot and sage leaves and saute for a further 8 minutes. Remove the mixture from the pan and set aside.

Turn the heat to medium-high, heat the flaxseed oil and fry the livers for 2 minutes on each side. Remove from the pan and set aside

Add the mustard and cognac to the pan and stir through. Return the vegetable mix to the pan and heat through.

Reduce the heat to low, stir through the cream and season to taste.

Return the livers to the pan and stir through to heat the livers.

Serve hot, garnished with the chopped parsley.

Green Salad

SERVES 8

175g (6oz) rocket leaves, rinsed and dried

2 medium avocados, chopped

2 small Lebanese cucumbers, chopped

2 tbsps capers, drained

¼ cup (60ml, 2fl oz) lemon juice

¼ cup (60ml, 2fl oz) olive oil

2 tbsps fresh parsley leaves, finely chopped

1 tsp red wine vinegar

½ tsp salt

Freshly ground pepper

Combine the rocket, avocado, cucumber and capers in a large salad bowl.

In a small bowl, whisk together the lemon juice, olive oil, parsley leaves, vinegar, salt and a couple of grinds of pepper.

Pour the dressing over the salad and toss to combine.

Wilted Baby Spinach Salad

SERVES 2

2 tsps olive oil

2 small onions, halved and sliced

2 cloves garlic, crushed

2 tsps balsamic vinegar

¼ tsp brown sugar

2 tbsps raisins

300g (10oz) baby spinach leaves, washed and drained

Pinch of salt

½ tsp lemon zest

1 orange, peeled and segmented, membranes removed

Freshly ground pepper to taste

Heat the oil in a medium frying pan over medium heat. Add the onion and garlic and saute for 15 minutes, until the onion has softened. Add the raisins, vinegar and brown sugar and stir through. Cook for a further 10 minutes, until the onion has caramelised. Add the spinach leaves in batches, until they are just wilted. Mix through the salt and lemon zest. Place in a large bowl with the orange segments. Toss to combine and season to taste. Serve warm.

ROCKET

Rocket might be the world's tastiest lettuce. A bright grass-green in colour, the leaves are slender, frilly, crisp and a little velvety in texture. Rocket is appropriately named — the flavour can be intensely peppery and sharp like a chive. Toss it into any salad or create a flavourful pesto with a blend of basil, rocket, pine nuts, olive oil, salt and pepper. Add the low-lactose, high-protein Parmesan cheese if eating dairy. The saucy, salty mix can be eaten by the spoonful or used as a marinade for a delicious meat roast.

Home-Made Blood Sausage

LEARN TO MAKE THIS EUROPEAN CLASSIC THAT'S PACKED FULL OF IRON AND DELICIOUS TOO

SERVES 6

700g (1½ lb) pearl barley

450g (1lb) pork fillet

250g (9oz) pork belly

2 cups (300g, 10oz) onion, chopped

3 tbsps fresh sage, chopped

¼ tsp nutmeg

2 tsps chilli powder

2 tsps caraway seeds

7 cups (1.75L, 3pt 11fl oz) blood (ask your local butcher)

12 sausage casings, 45cm (18in) long, thoroughly rinsed

Boil the barley in a large pot of salted water for 45 minutes until tender.

Cut the pork into chunks about 8mm thick. They need to fit easily into the casings while giving you a nice pork flavour.

Heat a large high-sided frying pan over medium-high heat and add the pork with a quarter cup of water. Cook for around 30 minutes until the fat is mostly liquid.

Add the onions and stir through. Cook for 10 minutes more until onions have browned.Stir through the sage, nutmeg, chilli and caraway.

Place in a large mixing bowl along with the barley and let the mixture cool to room temperature for 3 hours. If you proceed with the next step and the mix isn't cooled, it will ruin the whole process!

Gently mix the blood into the pork and barley mix. Don't do this roughly or you will create foam, which you don't want. Just before you stuff the sausages, put a large pot of water on the stove to simmer.

You will need a large funnel to stuff the sausage skins. Tie a secure knot in one end of the casing. Open the other end and place it over the end of the funnel.

Push the filling through the funnel into the sausage casing (it always helps to have a second person holding the casing to the funnel at this point). Fill the casing to just under three-quarters full only. Remove the end from the funnel, squeeze the casing together and tie a knot in the other end. Ensure there are no air pockets in the sausages before tying them off. Pinch the middle of the sausage together and then twist it in the middle.

Simmer the sausages for 15 minutes. Do not let the water boil. If the sausages float, there are probably air pockets. Pierce the air pockets, after cooking them for at least 5 minutes, to release the air.

Remove the sausages and allow them to dry. They can be stored in the fridge for up to 3 days.

To cook, roast the sausages in an oven for 40 minutes at 180°C (350°F, Gas Mark 5).

FERMENTATION

There are pickle fans, and then there are those who find tangy, vinegary gherkins a little foreign. Yet it's worth keeping an open mind as the world of fermentation is vast: along with pickles, for example, there are cultured foods, sauerkraut and kombucha, that cloudy bottled beverage that is currently in vogue.

An ancient method of preserving food for long seasons, fermentation is a chemical process that enhances a food's natural health benefits. It converts starches and sugars into lactic acid and produces the bacteria lactobacilli. These healthy bacteria, also known as 'probiotics', balance out bad bacterias in the gut and can prevent all sorts of digestive issues, boost the immune system and kick-start the metabolism.

THE BEST FERMENTED FOODS

- YOGHURT: Look for the term 'active cultures' on the label. Steer clear of flavoured yoghurts. Instead add stewed fruits, cinnamon, cocoa or dark chocolate flakes at home.
- KEFIR: Kefir is tarter and sourer than yoghurt and takes a bit more for the taste buds to get used to. Add it to a banana smoothie for starters.
- SAUERKRAUT: That vinegary, crunchy, sometimes spicy stuff that comes on the side of a pork roast, sauerkraut is fermented cabbage, usually seasoned with nutmeg or pepper, bay leaves, caraway seeds or fennel, all which add nutritional oomph.
- KIMCHI: A spicy Korean condiment and side dish made with Chinese cabbage, fermented in ginger, garlic, sugar, fish sauce and dried chilli flakes. It's flavour-packed with fibre, vitamins K and C, and iron.
- KOMBUCHA: This lightly fizzy, fermented tea tastes both bitter and tart and can be taken as a shot for an energy boost. There are oodles of brands now and the best ones are sugar-free, organic and use a slow fermentation process.
- CULTURED COTTAGE CHEESE: Look for 'active cultures' on the label, then lather this protein-packed gem onto raw vegetables or rice crackers.

DIY FERMENTING

- Combine vinegar, salt, sugar and water with seasonings like peppercorns, coriander, mustard, caraway, fennel or dill seeds.
- Bring to a boil and pour over vegetables in secure jars sterilized with boiling water.
- The mixture will bubble when it starts to ferment. The sour odour will give it away. Fermentation can take two weeks or longer.

Ginger Lemon Kombucha Tea

WHY NOT TRY MAKING YOUR OWN KOMBUCHA? IT'S CHEAPER, TASTIER AND MUCH MORE REWARDING THAN BUYING THE PRE-MADE DRINK

MAKES 2 LITRES

8 cups (2L, 4pt) water

16 teabags

2 cups (440g, 1lb) sugar

A SCOBY (starter culture)

3 tbsps fresh ginger, chopped

½ small lemon, sliced

Place water, teabags and sugar in a large saucepan over a medium-high heat and bring to the boil. Remove from the heat and allow to steep. Set aside until the tea has cooled to room temperature. (Hot tea will destroy the SCOBY.)

When tea has completely cooled pour it into a glass jar or kombucha urn.

With clean hands, gently place the SCOBY at the top of the jar or urn.

Cover the jar or urn with a muslin cloth and secure with an elastic band.

Put the jar in a warm corner of the kitchen and leave to ferment for 7 days.

Give it a 'second fermentation' by placing it with ginger and lemon in a bottled container at room temperature for 3 days.

Strain the kombucha through a fine mesh sieve into sealable jars and store in the fridge until ready to drink.

Transfer the SCOBY to a fresh batch of tea and start again!

Note: SCOBY stands for symbiotic culture of bacteria and yeast. You may be able to find it at a health-food store or farmers market. If not, try online.

Red and Green Cabbage Sauerkraut

SAUERKRAUT IS GREAT FOR YOUR GUT AND DIGESTIVE HEALTH, AND IT'S A REALLY HANDY ACCOMPANIMENT TO HAVE IN THE FRIDGE

MAKES 6 CUPS

½ green cabbage

½ red cabbage

3 tsps fine sea salt

1 tbsp fresh ginger, grated

2 cloves garlic, finely chopped

1 cup (250ml, 8fl oz) brine (1 tbsp of sea salt dissolved in 1 cup water)

1 tbsp fresh parsley leaves, finely chopped

Using a mandolin or box grater, separately shred the cabbage.

Transfer the cabbage to a large glass or ceramic bowl and sprinkle with sea salt. Mix to coat the cabbage and set aside for 10 minutes.

Next, using hands or a potato masher, squeeze the cabbage for 10 minutes to release all the natural moisture.

Pack the cabbage, ginger and garlic into a glass jar tightly to remove as many air pockets as possible.

Pour in the brine ensuring that vegetables are covered with about 2cm (1in) of water on top. If there is insufficient brine, add more water and salt in the same ratio.

Place a cheesecloth over the vegetables and secure it with a weighted object, such as a water-filled jar or heavy stone. Press down firmly to remove any remaining air pockets.

Cover the fermenting jar with a clean and dry tea towel and place it on a plate to capture any spillage.

Place the container in a dry place at room temperature and out of direct sunlight and leave to ferment for 5 to 7 days. Check daily to ensure the liquid still covers the vegetables.

Transfer to a glass jar and store in the fridge when ready.

Serve garnished with a sprinkling of fresh parsley.

ROSEMARY

Rosemary is a pretty, fragrant shrub with slim little leaves. It grows wild in warm, lush climates. It's a staple in Mediterranean cuisine and is a classic seasoning for cosy, hearty dishes as well as summery salads and appetizers. The flavour of a roast lamb transforms with a few sprigs of rosemary, and then the pungent, lemony taste can be used to infuse the vegetables — roasted carrots with rosemary are bright and gorgeous to eat. Rosemary is also an excellent seasoning to use for pickling vegetables.

Pickled Sprouts

MAKES 2.5 LITRES

1kg (2lb) Brussels sprouts, ends trimmed and halved lengthways

3 tbsps fresh parsley, finely chopped

5 cloves garlic, sliced

2 tbsps black peppercorns

5 cups (1.25L, 42fl oz) filtered water

5 cups (1.25L, 42fl oz) white wine vinegar

7 tbsps salt

Soak the sprouts in a large bowl filled with lightly salted water for 30 minutes, then drain. Clean and sterilize 5 x 500ml (1pt) canning jars by boiling them and lids in water for at least 5 minutes. Place sprouts in a large bowl and mix with the parsley, garlic and peppercorns then place in the jars, leaving a 1cm (½ in) gap from the top. Bring the filtered water, vinegar and salt to a boil in a large saucepan. Reduce the heat to low and simmer until the salt is dissolved. Pour the liquid into the jars until it just covers the sprouts. Gently shake the jars to encourage any trapped air bubbles to float to the top. Seal the jars and place them in a large pot of boiling water for 15 minutes. Let sit for 4 weeks before eating.

Pickled Zucchini

MAKES 2.5 LITRES

1kg (2lb) zucchinis, halved and sliced 5mm (¼ in) thick

5 cloves garlic, sliced

3 tbsps rosemary leaves

3 tbsps fresh chives, chopped

3 tbsps fresh thyme leaves, roughly chopped

1 tbsp mustard seeds

2 tbsps black peppercorns

5 cups (1.25L, 42fl oz) filtered water

5 cups (1.25L, 42fl oz) white wine vinegar

7 tbsps salt

Soak zucchini in a large bowl filled with lightly salted water for 30 minutes, then drain. Clean and sterilize 5 x 500ml (1pt) canning jars by boiling them and lids in water for at least 5 minutes. Place zucchini in a bowl and mix with garlic, rosemary, chives, thyme, mustard seeds and peppercorns then place in the jars, leaving a 1cm (½ in) gap from the top. Bring filtered water, vinegar and salt to a boil in a large saucepan. Reduce heat to low and simmer until the salt is dissolved. Pour the liquid into jars until it just covers the zucchini slices. Gently shake the jars, then seal and place in a large pot of boiling water for 15 minutes. Let sit for 4 weeks before eating.

Paleo Vegan Cookies

PACKED FULL OF NUTS, SEEDS AND FRUIT FOR HAPPY,
HEALTHY BODIES

MAKES 20

3 cups (375g, 13oz) raw pecans

½ cup (75g, 3oz) ground flaxseeds

¼ tsp sea salt

¼ cup (30g, 1oz) pepitas (pumpkin seeds)

1 cup (160g, 6oz) sultanas

¼ cup (40g, 1½ oz) sesame seeds

⅓ cup (80ml, 3fl oz) coconut oil, melted

⅓ cup (80ml, 3fl oz) water

½ cup (180g, 6oz) maple syrup

1 tbsp vanilla extract

Preheat oven to 180°C (350°F, Gas Mark 5). Line a large flat baking tray with baking paper.

Place the pecans in the food processor and process until a fine flour forms. Add the flaxseed and salt and pulse until just combined.

Add the oil, water, maple syrup and vanilla extract and process until thoroughly combined.

Transfer to a mixing bowl and stir in the pepitas, sultanas and sesame seeds.

Place a piece of baking paper on a clean work surface and use a rolling pin to roll out the dough to approximately 5mm (¼ in) thick. Use a cookie cutter to cut out circles of the dough.

Bake in the oven for 20 minutes, or until golden brown.

Let cool on a wire rack for 5 minutes before serving.

Vegetarian

BEING VEGETARIAN

It's a debate: is it healthy to be a vegetarian? Is it healthier than being a meat-eater? Vegetarian diets used to be joked about — 'It's rabbit food! There's only so much tofu a person can eat!' Yet, vegetarian cooking is being increasingly embraced by nutritionists and chefs who celebrate ways to get all the required protein and nutrients and enjoy the health benefits of leaving meat behind. (And it doesn't have to be strict: even going a few days a week without meat can make a difference.)

Vegetarian means a diet without meat. Vegan means a diet without animal products. Vegetarians eat cheese, milk and cream. Vegans do not.

There are many reasons why some nutritionists swear by a vegetarian diet, whether it's temporary or a permanent lifestyle change. A vegetarian diet can help kick-start weight loss or it can refresh the digestive system, especially after illnesses. Going vegetarian can help prevent or heal chronic illnesses, from heart conditions to chronic fatigue. In general, with healthy habits, vegetarian diets tend to be lower in fat and especially 'bad' fats. Studies show that vegetarian diets can be higher in vitamin C and fibre. An absence of meat reduces the risk of antibiotics and additives in meat entering the body.

When switching to a vegetarian diet it's essential to make up protein and iron, which are slightly easier to get from meat. Yet it doesn't have to be boring. A little research and planning go a long way.

TIPS FOR A VEGETARIAN DIET

- Avoid replacing meat with processed 'faux meat' products, which can contain sugar, saturated fat and, especially, sodium.
- Packaged and flavoured tofu is great but some brands are heavy with additives and preservatives. Fresh food is always healthier.
- There's protein everywhere, so you don't need to go without. Peas, lentils, seeds and nuts, tofu and whole grains like oats, quinoa and brown rice are all good sources. Beans are protein machines and they provide texture and yumminess in cooking. Rice and beans is a powerful combination of protein, fibre and many minerals. Serve it with guacamole and indulge!
- Eggs are a wonder food, full of protein, iron, vitamin B and D, and zinc for healthy skin and muscles. Get baking and scrambling.
- Be daring with vegetables. It seems obvious that vegetarians will eat a lot of vegetables, though it's less obvious that there are more delicious ways to prepare vegetables than meat. Blanch, steam, marinate, bake and barbecue. Mash and add seasonings. Blend and turn into burgers.

Roasted Capsicum Soup

A LIGHT LUNCH OR DINNER OPTION THAT WILL
FILL YOU UP BUT WON'T WEIGH YOU DOWN

SERVES 6

2 large red capsicums, quartered, seeds removed

2 large yellow capsicums, quartered, seeds removed

1/3 cup (80ml, 3fl oz) olive oil

1 medium onion, chopped

3 cloves garlic, minced

1 tsp ground cumin

1 tsp ground oregano

2 tbsps fresh coriander leaves

4 cups (1L, 2pt) vegetable stock

½ cup (125g, 4oz) Greek yoghurt

Salt and freshly ground black pepper

Preheat oven to 220°C (425°F, Gas Mark 7). Line a large flat baking tray with baking paper.

Place the capsicum quarters on the tray and drizzle over with half the olive oil.

Bake in the oven for at least 25 minutes, or until they start to blacken and the skin blisters.

Remove from the oven and seal them in a plastic bag for 15 minutes.

Once they are cool enough to handle, peel off the skins and roughly chop the flesh.

Heat the rest of the oil in a large pot over medium-high heat. Add the onion and garlic and saute for 5 minutes, until the onion is translucent.

Add the capsicum, cumin, oregano and coriander leaves and saute for a further 5 minutes.

Add the stock and bring to a boil. Then reduce the heat to low and simmer, covered, for 30 minutes.

Let cool for 10 minutes, then pour into a blender and puree until mostly blended.

Return to the pot, heat until just about to boil and stir through the yoghurt. Remove from the heat and season to taste with the salt and pepper.

Serve hot.

Roasted Stuffed Capsicums

SUBSTANTIAL, FILLING AND FLAVOURSOME, THIS COULD
BECOME ONE OF YOUR GO-TO VEGETARIAN RECIPES

SERVES 4

4 large red capsicums

20 vine cherry tomatoes

$^1/_3$ cup (80ml, 3fl oz) olive oil

2 medium onions, finely chopped

3 cloves garlic, minced

Freshly ground black pepper

300g (10oz) button mushrooms, chopped into 5mm (¼ in) cubes

1 large eggplant, chopped into 5mm (¼ in) cubes

100g (3½ oz) pine nuts

½ tsp salt

3 tbsps fresh mint leaves, shredded

100g (3½ oz) pitted kalamata olives, chopped

12 toothpicks, soaked in hot water for 30 minutes

Preheat oven to 200°C (400°F, Gas Mark 6).

Heat half the oil in a large frying pan over medium-high heat. Add the onion and garlic and saute for 5 minutes, until the onion has softened.

Add the mushrooms, eggplant and pine nuts to the pan and saute for a further 5 minutes.

Place the mushroom mixture into a large bowl and add the salt, a couple of grinds of pepper, mint and olives and toss to combine.

Slice into one side of the capsicum only and carefully remove the seeds without splitting the capsicums any further.

Stuff the capsicums with equal portions of the mushroom stuffing. Skewer the open edges with toothpicks to keep the capsicums together after you have stuffed them.

Place in a large baking dish with the tomatoes scattered around.

Drizzle with the remaining olive oil and roast in the oven for 35 minutes, or until the capsicum skins start to brown and blister.

Serve hot with the roasted tomatoes on the side.

Pumpkin and Spinach No-Pasta Lasagne

NO CARBS, NO DAIRY AND ALL FLAVOUR, THIS LASAGNE OPTION IS A GREAT ONE TO HAVE ON HAND FOR VEGAN DIETS

SERVES 4

4 tbsps olive oil

800g (1¾ lb) butternut pumpkin, cut into 5mm (¼ in) thick slices

TOMATO SAUCE

2 x 400g (14oz) can diced tomatoes

1 onion, chopped

3 cloves garlic, crushed

3 tbsps tomato paste

½ tsp raw sugar

2 tbsps fresh basil, chopped

3 tbsps fresh oregano, chopped

1 tsp salt

½ tsp pepper

SPINACH FILLING

¼ cup (10g, ¼ oz) fresh parsley leaves, chopped

500g (1lb 2oz) fresh baby spinach leaves, roughly chopped

Preheat oven to 190°C (375°F, Gas Mark 5). Line a large flat baking tray with baking paper.

Toss the pumpkin slices in a bowl together with half the olive oil and a pinch of salt and pepper.

Lay the slices out on the baking tray and bake in the oven for 20 minutes. Remove from the oven and set aside.

To make the sauce, heat the rest of the oil in a large frying pan over medium-high heat.

Add the onion and garlic and saute for 5 minutes, until the onion has softened.

Add the tomato paste and stir through for 1 minute. Add the diced tomatoes, sugar, basil, oregano, salt and pepper.

Cook for 15 minutes until the sauce has thickened and some of the liquid has boiled off.

Toss together the spinach leaves and parsley in a large bowl.

Lightly oil a 28 x 18cm (11 x 7in) deep-sided baking dish.

Spread ¼ cup of the tomato sauce on the bottom of the dish.

Layer half the pumpkin slices over the top. Place half the spinach and parsley leaves over this and then spread half the remaining tomato sauce over the top.

Repeat with the remaining pumpkin, spinach mix and tomato sauce.

Bake for 40 minutes.

Remove from the oven and let it cool for 10 minutes.

Serve hot, garnished with extra basil leaves.

Roasted Cauliflower Tacos with Chipotle-Tahini Sauce

WHO NEEDS MEAT WHEN YOU'VE GOT THE MIGHTY CAULIFLOWER, AND THE SMACK-BANG FLAVOURS OF CHIPOTLE AND TAHINI?

SERVES 4

CAULIFLOWER

1 large head cauliflower, broken into florets

3 tbsps coconut oil

1 tsp ground cumin

1 tsp ground coriander

1 tsp ground oregano

Salt and freshly ground black pepper

CHIPOTLE-TAHINI SAUCE

¼ cup (60g, 2oz) tahini

2 tbsps lime juice

1 dried jalapeño chilli, soaked in hot water for 20 minutes, then minced

1 tsp cayenne pepper

¼ cup (65g, 2oz) Greek yoghurt

1 tsp maple syrup

¼ tsp salt

¼ tsp freshly ground pepper

TACOS

12 small, round corn tortillas

4 radishes, thinly sliced

1 cup (45g, 1½ oz) coriander leaves, chopped

8 yellow cherry tomatoes, sliced

6 spring onions, sliced

¼ red cabbage, shredded

Preheat oven to 220°C (425°F, Gas Mark 7). Line a large flat baking tray with baking paper.

Toss the cauliflower in a large bowl with the coconut oil, spices and a pinch of salt and pepper. Place the florets on the baking tray and roast for 15 minutes. Remove and toss the florets, then return to the oven for a further 20 minutes, until the cauliflower has started to turn golden brown.

To make the sauce, whisk together the sauce ingredients in a medium bowl. Season to taste.

Heat the tortillas by dry-frying them for 1 minute on each side in a small frying pan over medium heat. Stack them on a warm plate and cover with a tea towel, while you're frying them.

Assemble your tacos by topping your tortillas with small amounts of cauliflower, radish, coriander leaves, tomatoes, spring onion and cabbage. Drizzle some chipotle-tahini sauce over the top and enjoy!

Zucchini Pasta with Sun-Dried Tomato Sauce

A VEGAN AND PALEO-FRIENDLY DINNER THAT'S CREAMY, NUTTY AND TANGY IN FLAVOUR

SERVES 4

6 large zucchinis

1 tbsp olive oil

½ cup (125ml, 4fl oz) coconut cream

½ cup (125ml, 4fl oz) filtered water

1 cup (55g, 2oz) semi-dried tomatoes, roughly chopped

¾ cup (90g, 3oz) hazelnuts, finely chopped

Small handful vegan Parmesan cheese, grated (optional)

Wash the zucchinis and then use a shredder or spiralizer to shred into long, thin strips, around the same size as spaghetti strands.

Gently squeeze the zucchini to remove excess water and pat dry with paper towels.

Heat the oil in a large frying pan over medium-high heat.

Add the zucchini strips and cook for 4 minutes, until heated through.

Add the coconut cream and water and cook for a further 3 minutes.

Add the tomatoes and hazelnuts and gently stir through for 2 minutes.

Transfer zucchini to a serving bowl. Toss through the Parmesan cheese.

Season with salt and pepper.

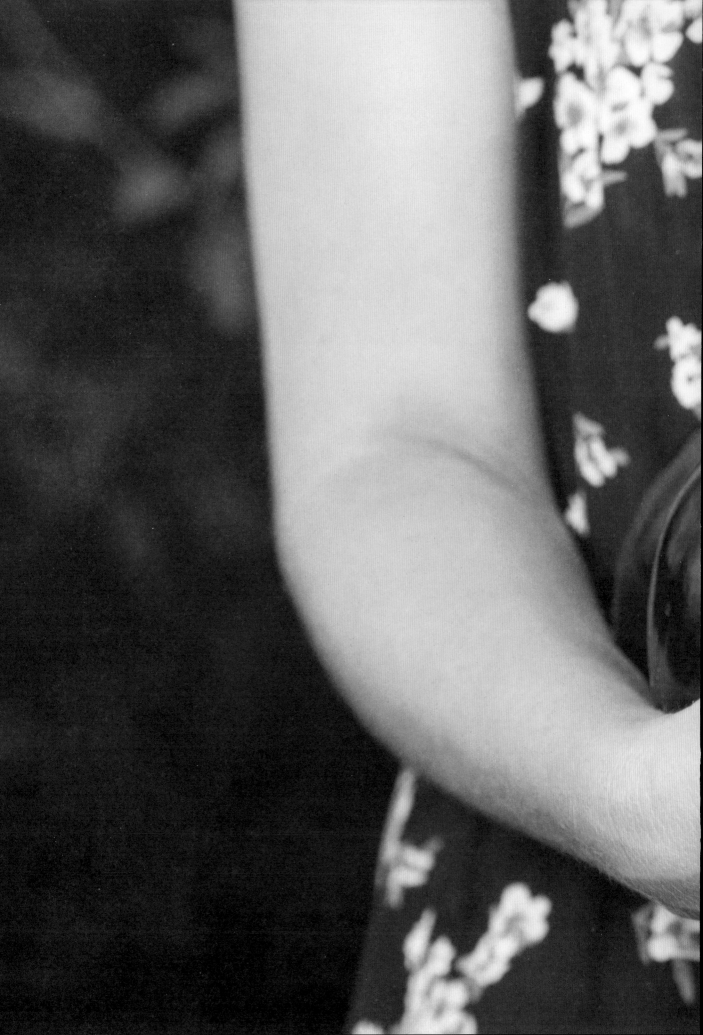

EGGPLANT

These shiny, purple-skinned vegetables that hang like lamps from leafy vines are celebrated for their nutritional goodness. There are over 700 varieties in the world — the Italian globe is popular, and Japanese and Chinese eggplants are also beloved.

Eggplant is a 'nightshade' vegetable, related to tomatoes, capsicums, chillies and potatoes, which are rich in antioxidants. The skin of an eggplant is pumping with nasunin, which is like a juice shot for the brain. It'll help that short-term memory! Nightshades can be problematic: while they help reduce inflammation in most people, the toxin they produce to protect themselves from insects can cause inflammation in others. Moderation is a good thing — enjoy those baked eggplant chips with tahini paste just once a week.

Eggplant is a sneaky substitute for meat. Grilled or barbecued, its flesh softens and becomes juicy, yet has a satisfying chew. Its gorgeous skin becomes silky and chewy. Cut eggplant into thick, round discs, and marinate before grilling. Layer it with lettuce, feta cheese and grilled onion for an amazing vegetarian burger. Use hummus rather than ketchup as the zesty, creamy condiment.

Eggplant makes a great alternative to meat lasagne and it's amazing in curry as it easily absorbs flavour. Also, eggplant can be transformed into vegetable fritters or fries with a light battering of whole-wheat flour. Serve with yoghurt dip spiced with paprika or cumin.

BABA GANOUSH

Baba ganoush is eggplant's standout dish. Eaten like peanut butter throughout the Mediterranean, it is super-simple to make. Avoid recipes that include fatty ingredients like cream cheese; the eggplant is rich and textured enough to hold the dip together. A little bit of yoghurt is a healthy dose of dairy, and tahini, the sesame taste, provides protein. Lemon juice, parsley, salt and pepper provide all the zesty, balancing flavours needed. Baba ganoush can be smoothed onto bread instead of butter and is a lemony dip that's lower in fat than hummus.

COOKING TIP

USE SALT: If there is an extra 30 minutes before cooking, it's a good idea to rinse the eggplant and sprinkle it with salt. This reduces bitterness and toughness, and soaks up moisture, so that when sauteed, roasted or fried, the flesh transforms into whatever texture is desired — firm, silky, juicy or crunchy. A salted eggplant will absorb less grease when fried to create a lighter, healthier treat.

Stuffed Eggplants with Pistachio Crumble

FLAVOUR IS A GIVEN, BUT IT'S THE TEXTURES OF THIS DISH THAT DELIGHT: GOOEY CHEESE, CRUNCHY NUTS AND TENDER EGGPLANT

SERVES 4

2 large eggplants, halved lengthways

CRUMBLE

½ cup (60g, 2oz) roasted pistachios, roughly chopped

¾ cup (90g, 3oz) fresh breadcrumbs (or use quinoa flakes)

1 tsp salt flakes

150g (5oz) mozzarella, torn into shreds

¼ cup (50ml, 2fl oz) olive oi

TOMATO SAUCE

3 tbsps olive oil

1 large onion, chopped

2 cloves garlic, crushed

2 large ripe tomatoes, chopped

1 tbsp tomato paste

¼ cup (60g, 2oz) tomato passata

1 tsp dried mixed herbs

½ tsp salt

¼ cup (10g, ¼ oz) fresh basil leaves, plus extra for garnish

Preheat oven to 200°C (400°F, Gas Mark 6). Lightly oil a 28 x 18cm (11 x 7in) deep-sided baking dish.

Using a sharp knife, scoop out the flesh from the inside of the eggplant halves, leaving a 1cm-thick (½ in) layer inside the halves.

Chop the eggplant flesh into small 5mm (¼ in) cubes.

To make the tomato sauce, heat the oil in a medium-sized frying pan over medium-high heat. Add the onion and garlic and saute for 4 minutes, until the onion is translucent.

Add the tomatoes, tomato paste, passata, chopped eggplant flesh, dried herbs, salt and basil leaves and cook for a further 15 minutes, until the eggplant is softened.

Spoon the cooked tomato mix in equal portions back into the eggplant halves.

Layer the mozzarella over the top, then sprinkle over the breadcrumbs, pistachios and salt.

Place the halves in the baking dish and drizzle over the olive oil.

Bake for 30 minutes, or until the mozzarella is melted and the breadcrumbs are golden brown.

Serve with extra basil leaves for garnish.

Eggplant Pate

MAKES 1 CUP

1 large eggplant

2 tbsps olive oil

1 small onion, quartered and sliced

2 cloves garlic, crushed

2 small red chillies, seeded and finely sliced

¼ cup (30g, 1oz) walnuts, roughly chopped

1 tsp salt

1 tsp ground coriander

1 tsp ground cumin

¼ tsp cayenne pepper

½ tbsp rosemary leaves, finely chopped

Grill eggplant over an open flame. When skin begins to blacken place in a sealed plastic bag for 15 minutes. Once cool, peel off skin and roughly chop flesh. Heat oil in a large frying pan over medium heat. Add onion, garlic and chillies and saute for 10 minutes, until onion is soft. Add eggplant flesh and walnuts and cook for 15 minutes, until eggplant is breaking apart. Add salt, spices and half the rosemary and stir through for 2 more minutes. Mash the mixture until it is a thick sauce consistency. Season to taste and serve warm, garnished with the rest of the rosemary leaves and a side of crusty bread

Eggplant Chips & Tomato Sauce

SERVES 4

3 large eggplants

2 tbsps salt flakes

3 tbsps olive oil

2 tsps dried mixed herbs

SAUCE

¼ cup (60ml, 2fl oz) olive oil

1 x 400g (14oz) can crushed tomatoes

4 cloves garlic, minced

1 tsp chilli flakes

1 tsp cayenne pepper

½ tsp salt

¼ tsp brown sugar

Slice eggplant into wedges and toss in a bowl with half the salt; sit for 30 minutes. Preheat oven to 200°C (400°F, Gas Mark 6). Line baking tray with baking paper. Squeeze eggplant to remove liquid and pat dry. Toss with olive oil, remaining salt and herbs. Place in even layer on baking tray and bake for 1 hour, turning halfway. Heat ¼ cup olive oil in a small saucepan. Add garlic, chilli and cayenne and fry for 2 minutes. Add tomatoes, salt and sugar. Bring to boil, then reduce heat and simmer for 15 minutes until sauce thickens. Puree in blender until smooth. Serve chips with dipping sauce.

OLIVE OIL

A good olive oil is essential to have on hand. Drizzle it over eggplant before sauteing or barbecuing, and the evening is sure to go well. Marinating eggplant in olive oil then slow-roasting it in the oven is a chef's trick for preserving the lush, hearty vegetable — chefs call it 'confit', which is the word for an animal cooking in its own fat (usually applied to a duck in French cooking). The process draws out layers of texture and flavour, so that eggplants morph from fluffy to chewy to silky and meaty. Things gets really tasty when garlic and chilli are added to the mix.

Roasted Eggplant, Spinach and Quinoa Salad with Miso Dressing

SOFT, LUSCIOUS EGGPLANT AND CRUNCHY QUINOA MAKE FOR A GREAT SALAD COMBINATION

SERVES 4

4 small eggplants, cut into 1cm-thick (½ in) slices

2 tbsps olive oil

½ tsp salt

1½ cups (255g, 9oz) uncooked quinoa, rinsed

3 cups (750ml, 24fl oz) vegetable stock

1 tsp red miso paste

1 cup (250ml, 8fl oz) warm water

1 tbsp black sesame seeds

2 tsps sesame oil

1 tsp tamari

2 bird's-eye chillies, seeds removed, sliced

50g (2oz) baby spinach, washed and dried

3 spring onions, sliced

½ cup (10g, ¼ oz) fresh coriander leaves

Preheat oven to 230°C (450°F, Gas Mark 8). Line a large flat baking tray with baking paper.

Heat a small frying pan over medium-high heat and dry-fry the sesame seeds for 2 minutes or until they begin to brown. Remove immediately from the pan and set aside.

Toss the eggplant slices with 1 tablespoon of olive oil and salt. Lay out the slices on the baking tray and bake for 25 minutes or until the eggplant slices are browned, turning halfway through.

Mix the miso paste with the warm water. Strain through a small sieve to remove any grains. Stir the sesame seeds, sesame oil, tamari and sliced chillies into the strained liquid and set aside.

To cook the quinoa, bring the quinoa and stock to the boil in a large saucepan. Reduce the heat, cover and let it simmer for 20 minutes, or until quinoa is cooked.

Heat the rest of the olive oil in a medium saucepan over medium heat. Add the spinach and spring onion and cook until the spinach is wilted. Remove from the heat and mix with the quinoa.

To serve, place the roasted eggplant slices over a bed of quinoa and spinach.

Drizzle over the dressing and garnish with coriander leaves.

TOFU

Tofu is made from mature white soybeans that have been churned into milk, which is then boiled, curdled, pressed, soaked, separated and transformed back into many different forms of tofu.

There are tofu lovers and then there are hard-core carnivores who might wonder why bother? It's true that the jiggly white substance has very little flavour when cooked up on its own. Yet tofu is easy to eat and soybeans have a beautiful balance of protein, amino acids, fats, carbohydrates, vitamins and minerals. This is part of the reason tofu is such an easy food to adopt when flirting with the idea of going vegetarian. And there have been many a tofu sceptic converted as chefs get creative, transforming tofu into spicy, sweet, earthy, saucy, crunchy, fried delicacies as the foodie world evolves and continues to embrace the vegetarian and vegan philosophies.

The difference in types of tofu is basically in texture. It comes in extra firm, firm, soft and silken. Each has unique qualities for cooking and tasting.

EXTRA FIRM

This is the meatiest tofu there is. It is excellent for frying and can become chewy and very flavoursome after marinating. Fry as it is, or lightly batter before frying, then get creative with the dipping sauces.

FIRM

When in doubt, buy firm tofu. It can be fried, battered or stir-fried without crumbling or becoming mushy. And it can also be eaten raw — it is lightly salty and a little bit woody.

SOFT

Soft tofu absorbs flavours gently — imagine a berry custard or a light ice cream flavoured with almonds and honey. It can be eaten cooked or raw, cut into cubes and thrown into a salad with any dressing. Raw, it has a mild, milky taste. Soft tofu is also great in soup; it takes on the flavour of the broth, yet provides gentle, textured bites.

SILKEN

Light, shiny and the texture of silk, this tofu can turn an average smoothie into a protein powerhouse. It is the basis for Asian desserts, such as the classic silken tofu with ginger syrup, or whipped up with vanilla and spooned over fresh mango. Silken tofu can be scrambled like eggs, served with avocado and beans. It will also turn a salad dressing into a meal — season it with lemon juice and dill or soy sauce, rice wine vinegar and ginger, shake and pour over a big bowl of mixed lettuce.

Eggplant Tofu Teriyaki

THIS GORGEOUS STICKY SAUCE IS PACKED FULL OF FLAVOUR
AND EXUDES TANTALIZING ASIAN AROMAS

SERVES 4

500g (1lb) firm tofu

2 tsps peanut oil

500g (1lb) eggplant, cut
into 2cm (1in) cubes

300g (10oz) shitake
mushrooms, sliced

2 cloves garlic, crushed

2 tbsps chives, chopped

1 tsp sesame seeds

Cooked rice, to serve

TERIYAKI SAUCE

½ tsp cornflour

¹/₃ cup (80ml, 3fl oz)
water

¼ cup (60ml, 2fl oz)
tamari (or soy sauce)

¼ cup (60ml, 2fl oz)
mirin

3 tbsps maple syrup

1 tbsp fresh ginger,
grated

2 cloves garlic, crushed

2 tsps sesame oil

To make the sauce, whisk the cornflour together with
1 tablespoon of the water in a small bowl, then stir in the rest of
the sauce ingredients. Set aside.

Pat dry the tofu with paper towels, pressing firmly to remove
excess liquid, then cut into 2cm (1in) cubes.

In a large wok, heat 1 teaspoon of the peanut oil over high heat.
Stir-fry the tofu for 5 minutes, until golden brown on the edges.
Remove from the wok and set aside.

Heat the rest of the oil and add the eggplant, mushrooms and
garlic and stir-fry for 3 minutes. Reduce the heat to medium and
stir for another 5 minutes until the eggplant has softened.

Give the sauce a quick whisk and pour into the wok. Heat until
bubbling and thickened. Return the tofu to the wok and heat
through for 2 minutes.

Serve the vegetables garnished with chives and sesame seeds and
with a side of rice.

Crispy Baked Tofu with Wild Rice and Mango

THIS FLAVOURSOME AND WHOLESOME BOWL TICKS OFF EVERY MAJOR
FOOD GROUP, ENSURING YOU FEEL FULL AND SATISFIED

SERVES 4

RICE

$^1/_3$ cup (50g, 2oz) wild
black rice

$^1/_3$ cup (50g, 2oz) red
rice

$^1/_3$ cup (50g, 2oz) brown
basmati rice

2¼ cups (560ml, 1pt
3fl oz) water

VEGETABLES

1 Lebanese cucumber,
peeled, seeded and
sliced

200g (7oz) sugar snap
peas, ends trimmed

1 cup (165g, 6oz) fresh
mango, cut into cubes

1 red onion, finely
chopped

¼ cup (30g, 1oz)
roasted peanuts,
roughly chopped

TOFU

500g (1lb) firm tofu

2 tbsps cornflour

½ tsp salt flakes

Freshly ground black
pepper

Olive oil cooking spray

DRESSING

$^1/_3$ cup (70ml, 2½ fl oz)
soy sauce

2 tbsps coriander
leaves, chopped

1 tbsps sesame oil

½ tsp chilli powder

Preheat oven to 200°C (400°F, Gas Mark 6). Line a large flat
baking tray with baking paper.

To cook the rice, bring the rices and water to the boil in a
large saucepan. Reduce the heat, cover and let it simmer for 40
minutes, or until the rice is cooked. Set aside to cool slightly.

Pat dry the tofu with paper towels, pressing firmly to remove
excess liquid, then cut into 2cm (1in) cubes. Toss with the
cornflour, salt and a couple of good grinds of pepper.

Place the tofu on the baking tray and spray with the olive oil.

Bake for 15 minutes, turning halfway. The tofu should become
golden brown and crisp.

While the tofu is baking, place the cucumber, peas, mango, onion
and peanuts in a large bowl with the cooked rice and toss to
combine.

To make the dressing, mix together the soy sauce, coriander
leaves, sesame oil and chilli powder in a small bowl.

Pour the dressing over the rice and vegetables and gently stir
through.

Serve the rice and vegetable mix with the tofu cubes scattered
over the top.

Cauliflower Mash with Tofu

SERVES 2

225g (8oz) firm tofu

Pinch of salt

Freshly ground black pepper

1 tbsp cornflour

Olive oil cooking spray

1 cup (125g, 4oz) raw cashews

1 medium head cauliflower, cut into florets

1 clove garlic

1 tbsp olive oil

2 tbsps water

1 tbsp fresh parsley, chopped

Place cashews in a bowl and cover with water. Set aside to soak for 1 hour. Drain and rinse. Pat tofu dry, pressing to remove excess liquid, then cut into cubes. Toss with cornflour, salt and pepper. Place tofu on baking tray and spray with olive oil. Bake for 15 minutes until golden, turning halfway. Cook cauliflower for 6 minutes in salted boiling water. Drain then place cauliflower in food processor with garlic, oil, water and cashews and process until creamy with the texture of mashed potato. Serve tofu on top of the cauliflower mash, garnished with parsley.

Stuffed Sweet Potato

SERVES 4

2 large sweet potatoes, washed

2 tsps coconut oil

2 large onions, chopped

3 cloves garlic, crushed

1 tbsp cayenne pepper

1 red capsicum, chopped

1 yellow capsicum, chopped

2 large tomatoes, chopped

1½ cups (300g, 10oz) cooked brown lentils

2 tbsps fresh oregano leaves, chopped

2 tsps salt

1 tbsp balsamic vinegar

¼ cup (65g, 2oz) Greek yoghurt

Preheat oven to 180°C (350°F, Gas Mark 4). Cut potatoes in half lengthways and place on baking tray, cut side down; bake for 40 minutes. Cool for 15 minutes, then scoop out most of the flesh. Heat oil in frying pan then add onion, garlic and cayenne and fry for 5 minutes. Add capsicums and tomato and cook for a further 5 minutes. In a bowl, combine potato flesh, lentils, tomato and capsicum mix, oregano leaves, salt and vinegar. Fill potato halves with the mixture. Return to the oven and bake for 15 minutes. Serve with yoghurt.

GARLIC CHIVE FLOWERS

Garlic chives are naturally intense — they belong to the onion family and have the potency of garlic, yet come in petite, elegant strands so somehow never overpower. And those deep-green strands bloom with soft white flowers that taste even more like garlic and look beautiful immersed in rice wine vinegar in a glass jar — this then creates a marinade for tofu, potato salads and vegetables. Many Asian stir-fry recipes call for garlic chives before the flower has blossomed — they do wonders in just a simple combination of tofu, mushrooms and ginger. When the flowers are available, throw a few on, even if just for decoration.

LEGUMES

Legumes are a staple in many cuisines. A little goes a long way, both for the earth and for the cultures that eat them — legumes grow easily and sustainably in dry places, and just a cup can be the core of a nutritious meal for a small family. For vegetarians, legumes are a saviour.

SO WHAT ARE THEY?

The most common legumes are beans: kidney, cannellini and black beans. Peas, certain nuts and lentils are also legumes. Legumes are tiny fruits that grow inside a pod, usually in grass-like crops. For eating, they equally balance protein, fat and carbohydrates.

There's one little trick: nutritionists recommend adding seeds or grains to legumes to make a 'complete protein', which means a meal that contains all the strength and energy that your body needs. Legumes have eight of the nine crucial amino acids that make up a complete protein; the ninth acid comes from a grain or a seed. Together these can be survived on for long periods. A classic combination that delivers this is hummus, which combines chickpeas (a legume) with tahini, which is a paste made out of sesame seeds. Another option: when cosying up with a bowl of lentil soup, mop it up with a slice of seeded, wholegrain bread.

SOME IMPORTANT LEGUMES

BEANS: Kidney beans, soybeans, fava beans and lima beans. Beans are high in protein and low in fat. They are also high in carbohydrates and so are recommended in small portions, especially when weight loss is the goal. However, with the energy boost, a long walk or a run may come naturally.

LENTILS: A lentil feast is high in fibre, protein, magnesium … and also super-colourful. Orange, red, white, yellow, green: there are oodles of types of lentils and they add bursts of colour when displayed in glass jars (airtight to keep them fresh). Rinse lentils first before cooking. And don't hold back on the creativity — most cuisines use them and there are so many recipes to experiment with.

NUTS: Peanuts and soy nuts are actually legumes, not nuts. Both are protein powerhouses that pack in carbohydrates and mostly healthy fats, so are best eaten in small portions. Go for dry-roasted and unsalted brands to skip the high fat and sodium of oil-roasted, salted nuts.

PEAS: Green peas, snow peas, snap peas, split peas and black-eyed peas — these are also high in carbohydrates and protein, yet have so little fat that they make for a very healthy choice.

Coconut Lentil Curry

GUARANTEED TO WARM YOU UP AND KEEP YOU SATISFIED
ON COLD WINTER EVENINGS

SERVES 4

2 tsps coconut oil

1 large onion, finely chopped

6 cloves garlic, minced

1 tsp brown mustard seeds

1 tsp turmeric

1 tsp ground coriander

1 tsp curry powder

2 tsps cumin

1¼ tsps salt

1 x 400ml (14fl oz) can coconut milk

¼ cup (150g, 5oz) tomato paste

4 cups (1L, 2pt) boiling water

1½ cups (275g, 9oz) uncooked brown lentils, rinsed

1½ cups (235g, 7oz) jasmine rice

1 tbsp ghee

4 naan bread

1 lime, quartered

Fresh coriander, chopped, to garnish

Heat oil in a saucepan on low-medium heat. Add onion and cook, stirring occasionally, until golden brown, approximately 5 minutes. Add garlic and fry for 1–2 minutes until the strong aroma disappears. Next add the brown mustard seeds and cook for 1–2 minutes until they pop. Then add turmeric, coriander, curry powder, cumin and salt and cook for another 30 seconds, stirring frequently.

Pour in the coconut milk, tomato paste, water and lentils and stir to combine. Bring to a boil, cover and cook on a low heat for 45 minutes.

Rinse the rice and place in 3 cups of cold water in a medium-sized pot. Bring to a boil, then reduce the heat to low and simmer, covered for 12 minutes. Stir once, halfway through. Remove from the heat and leave covered until ready to serve.

Heat half the ghee in a frying pan over medium heat. Fry the naan bread for 2 minutes on each side. Place on a warmed plate and cover with a tea towel while cooking the rest.

Season the curry to taste and garnish with chopped coriander. Serve with lime wedges, a side of rice and naan.

Red Lentil Soup

IT'S A LOOKS-GOOD, TASTES-GOOD, FEELS-GOOD SOUP IF EVER THERE WAS ONE

SERVES 6

2 tbsps coconut oil

1 large onion, chopped

4 cloves garlic, minced

2 tsps ground cumin

2 tsps ground oregano

2 tsps curry powder

1 bird's-eye chilli, seeds removed, finely chopped

2 x 400g (14oz) cans crushed tomatoes

450g (1lb) red lentils, rinsed

4 cups (1L, 2pt) vegetable stock

Salt, to taste

Freshly ground black pepper, to taste

1 egg yolk

¼ cup (60ml, 2fl oz) lemon juice

2 tbsps chopped fresh chives

Heat the oil in a large pot over medium-high heat. Add the onion and garlic and saute for 5 minutes, until the onion is translucent.

Add the cumin, oregano, curry and chilli and fry for 1 minute.

Stir through the tomatoes and bring to a boil. Reduce the heat and let it simmer for 10 minutes.

Add the lentils and stock and stir well. Bring to a boil and then reduce the heat to low. Cover and let it simmer for 30 minutes.

Season the soup to taste.

Mix ¼ cup of the soup with ¼ cup cold water. Then slowly mix together with the egg yolk. Pour the mixture back into the soup and stir well.

Let it simmer for another 15 minutes. The lentils should be completely softened by now and falling apart. If not, cook for another 10 minutes.

Add the lemon juice and then place the soup in a blender or use a stick blender to blend to a smooth puree.

Serve hot with fresh chives as a garnish.

Warm Potato Salad

SERVES 6

700g (1½ lb) baby potatoes, scrubbed

1 small head cauliflower, broken into small florets

1 tbsp coconut oil

1 tbsp salt flakes

½ tsp turmeric

250g (9oz) broad beans, skins removed (can use frozen)

4 spring onions, sliced

$^1/_3$ cup (80ml, 3fl oz) water

$^1/_3$ cup (85g, 3oz) Greek yoghurt

1 tbsps lemon juice

Salt and freshly ground black pepper

Preheat oven to 180°C (350°F, Gas Mark 5). Place cauliflower in bowl with half the coconut oil, salt and turmeric and toss to coat. Place on baking tray and bake for 20 minutes. Boil potatoes in pot of salted water for 15 minutes, until softened. Drain and sit for 10 minutes. Heat water and a pinch of salt in a small frying pan over medium heat and add the broad beans. Cover and cook for 3 minutes. Remove from heat. Cut potatoes in half and toss in a large bowl with cauliflower, beans and spring onions. Whisk together yoghurt and lemon juice and season with salt and pepper. Serve the warm vegetables with the sauce drizzled over.

Broad Bean Hummus

SERVES 4

450g (1lb) fresh broad beans, skins removed (can use frozen)

100g (3½ oz) cooked chickpeas

2 cloves garlic, minced

2½ tbsps tahini

1½ tbsps lemon juice

½ tsp salt

¼ tsp ground cumin

¼ tsp ground coriander

4 tbsps olive oil

¼ cup (60ml, 2fl oz) vegetable stock

Salt and pepper

Boil the beans in a pot of salted water for 2 minutes. Drain and rinse in cold water until they're cooled. Reserve 5 beans for garnish. Place the beans and the rest of the hummus ingredients, except for the stock and olive oil, in a blender. Process until smooth, slowly pouring in small amounts of stock and oil until the hummus is at your preferred consistency. Season to taste. Serve with the reserved beans, mint and sesame seeds sprinkled on top as well as a dusting of paprika and a good drizzle of olive oil.

BROAD BEANS

Also known as fava beans, these little gems punch above their weight as a source of lean protein, fibre and essential minerals and vitamins. They are only in season for a short time so keep an eye out for the green pods that can be eaten pod, bean and all. For larger pods, however, it's better to remove the outer skin of the pod and just eat the bean within. Some people prefer to blanch the bean, and remove the sometimes-tough skin to uncover the bright green slippery bean inside, as a precursor to cooking or eating raw. This is fiddly but some say well worth it.

Warm Roasted Vegetable Salad with Herb Dressing

THIS BRIGHT, COLOURFUL AND SUBSTANTIAL SALAD IS GREAT AS A SIDE DISH OR AS A MEAL IN ITSELF

SERVES 6

3 cups (300g, 10oz) Brussels sprouts, ends trimmed, and halved lengthways

1 large head of cauliflower, broken into florets

3 tbsps coconut oil

1 tsp salt

2 tsps lemon zest

1 large butternut pumpkin, peeled, seeded, and cut into 2cm (1in) cubes

3 tbsps maple syrup

½ tsp ground cinnamon

1 x 400g (14oz) can butter beans, drained and rinsed

200g (7oz) baby rocket leaves

3 tbsp roasted pepitas (pumpkin seeds)

Salt and pepper

HERB DRESSING

1 tbsp olive oil

2 tsps lemon juice

¾ cup (185g, 6oz) Greek yoghurt

1 tbsp fresh parsley, chopped

Preheat oven to 200°C (400°F, Gas Mark 6). Line 2 large flat baking trays with baking paper.

In a medium bowl, combine the Brussels sprouts and cauliflower, 2 tablespoons of coconut oil, salt and lemon zest and toss to combine. Spread out onto one of baking trays.

Toss the pumpkin cubes with the rest of the oil, the maple syrup and cinnamon and spread on a tray.

Roast the vegetables for 15 minutes, then remove from oven and turn them over and roast for a further 25 minutes, until they are all softened and browned.

In a large bowl, combine the roast vegetables with the rocket leaves, beans and pepitas.

To make the dressing, blend the ingredients together in a blender or using a stick blender until the parsley is combined.

Season to taste.

Serve the roasted vegetables warm with the dressing on the side.

Pumpkin and Chickpea Burger with the Lot

A HEALTHY AND TASTY BURGER OPTION THAT WILL KEEP YOU AND THE WHOLE FAMILY FULL FOR HOURS

SERVES 6

SALSA

4 tbsps olive oil

½ onion, chopped

2 cloves garlic, minced

½ bunch parsley, finely chopped

2 x 400g (14oz) cans chopped tomatoes

½ tsp brown sugar (optional)

BURGER PATTIES

Olive oil, for frying

1 onion, chopped

1 clove garlic, crushed

2 zucchinis, grated

1 carrot, grated

1 cup (225g, 8oz) cooked butternut pumpkin

¼ cup (30g, 1oz) breadcrumbs

1 x 400g (14oz) can chickpeas, rinsed and drained

3 tsps curry paste

3 tbsps crunchy peanut butter

1 egg yolk

¼ cup (10g, ¼ oz) coriander leaves, chopped

FILLING

6 bread rolls

½ cup (125g, 4oz) mayonnaise

2 tbsps sweet chilli sauce

1 cup (30g, 1oz) fresh baby spinach

½ cup (90g, 3oz) avocado, mashed

2 large tomatoes, sliced

12 yellow cherry tomatoes, sliced

1 cup (180g, 6oz) grilled zucchini slices

1 cup (175g, 6oz) grilled broccoli florets

½ cup (10g, ¼ oz) coriander leaves

To make the salsa, heat oil in a large frying pan over medium-high heat. Saute onion for 5 minues, until soft. Add garlic and saute for a further 1–2 minutes. Add parsley, tomatoes and sugar, if using. Reduce heat to a gentle simmer and cook for 10 minutes, until thickened.

To make the burger patties, heat oil in a large frying pan over medium-low heat. Add the onion and cook for 5 minutes, until softened. Add garlic, zucchini and carrot, and cook, stirring, for 3 minutes until softened. Drain off excess liquid.

Place breadcrumbs and chickpeas in the bowl of a food processor and pulse to combine. Add the vegetables, pumpkin, curry paste, peanut butter, egg yolk and coriander. Process until mixture comes together.

Form the mixture into 6 patties. Place in the fridge to chill for 15 minutes. Heat oil in a large frying pan over medium heat and cook the burgers, in batches, for 2 minutes each side until golden.

To make the chilli mayo sauce, whisk together the mayonnaise and the sweet chilli sauce in a small bowl.

Slice open the bread rolls and line the bottom half with baby spinach, then salsa, then avocado. Add the patty and then top with a good dollop of chilli mayo, then layer with red and yellow tomato, zucchini slices, broccoli and coriander. Gently press the top half of the bun over the patty.

Comfort Food

COMFORT FOOD

Once upon a time, eating healthily meant missing out on a lot of the fun. Not anymore. Often, changing the diet is about creating new healthy habits, which can be just as addictive and a lot better for the body and soul. Keeping an eye on levels of sugar and fat being consumed does not mean that there can't be pizza and movie night with chocolate mousse for dessert. There are myriad ways to turn comfort food into healthy comfort food.

PIZZA FOR DINNER

Here's a meaty surprise: how about chicken pizza crusts? Mix minced chicken with finely grated mozzarella, salt and pepper, then form into mini pizza circles and bake until the chicken is just cooked through. It's already delicious. Top with chopped onions, fresh tomatoes, basil and more mozzarella, then throw under the grill to bubble and brown.

Or, go vego and make a crust out of cauliflower florets. Break up the florets and place in a blender or food processor. Process until they form a rice-like consistency. Add grated mozzarella and Parmesan cheeses, egg, and oregano and garlic for seasoning. Bake it like a pizza, top with fresh tomato sauce, olives and parsley. Voila.

ZOODLES

In case you've missed it, noodles made out of vegetables is a thing these days. Use a spiralizer to cut large zucchinis into long, thin, curly strips and quickly saute in olive oil and pepper, until they're just a bit crunchy. Then toss in a healthy tomato sauce, or mushrooms, lemon and olive oil. It's a pasta dish like no other.

Wide zucchini strips can be used to create cannelloni for Italian feasts. Or go Mexican and make enchiladas: gently stream the zucchini and wrap the strips around grilled chicken or grilled vegetables and guacamole. Garnish with parsley.

AVOCADO

This bread-free sandwich is totally delicious: Cut an avocado in half and scoop the smooth halves intact from skin. Layer tomato slices, lettuce and some indulgent bacon on one half, then sandwich it with the other: an American BLT with a healthy twist.

A healthy chocolate mousse can be made completely dairy-free, using avocados for creaminess and cacao powder for the rich chocolate flavour. Indulge in maple syrup and vanilla extract for fragrance. This mousse can be quite powerful — add dashes of coconut milk to mellow it out.

Chickpea and Zucchini Rissole with Sprouted Greens

THE HEALTHIEST, HIPPEST BURGER IN TOWN — AND YOU
DON'T NEED TO WAIT AROUND AT A FOOD TRUCK FOR IT

SERVES 4

PATTIES

2 x 400g (14oz) cans
chickpeas, rinsed and
drained

3 small zucchinis,
coarsely grated and
squeezed to remove
excess moisture

1 cup (125g, 4oz)
breadcrumbs

1 cup (45g, 1½ oz)
fresh coriander, finely
chopped

3 cloves garlic, minced

3 tsps ground cumin

¼ tsp turmeric powder

1 egg, lightly beaten

3 tsps coconut oil

TO SERVE

4 organic sourdough
rolls

1 Lebanese cucumber,
halved and sliced
lengthways

2 cups (60g, 2oz) fresh
salad leaves

2 cups (100g, 3½ oz)
alfalfa sprouts

1 lemon, cut into
wedges

Place the chickpeas, zucchini, breadcrumbs, ¼ cup of the
coriander, garlic, cumin, turmeric and egg in a food processor.

Blend until almost smooth. If the mixture is too thick, add a
tablespoon of water at a time until the desired consistency. It
should be a thick mixture that you can shape easily.

Divide into 4 large burger patties.

Heat the coconut oil in a large frying pan over medium-high
heat.

Add the patties and fry for 5 minutes on each side until golden
brown.

To assemble the burgers, lightly toast the rolls and layer the salad
leaves, a slice of cucumber, a tablespoon of coriander and then
the burger on the bottom half of the roll.

At this point squeeze some lemon juice over the burger if you
like.

Place the alfalfa sprouts, then more salad leaves and cucumber
over the burger and place the other half of the roll on top.

Roast Turkey Breast with Potatoes and Cranberries

A HEALTHY, FRESH TAKE ON THE TRADITIONAL TURKEY ROAST WITH CRANBERRY SAUCE

SERVES 6

12 baby potatoes, peeled and halved

6 onions, halved

6 carrots, cut into 4cm (1½ in) sections

1 apple, cored and cut into quarters

2 lemons, quartered

¼ cup (60ml, 2fl oz) olive oil

1.5kg (3lb 5oz) turkey breasts

1 orange, zested

1 cup (100g, 3½ oz) fresh cranberries

¼ cup (10g, ¼ oz) fresh rosemary, chopped

2 tbsps fresh sage, chopped

Salt and pepper

Preheat oven to 230°C (450°F, Gas Mark 8).

Together in a large bowl, toss the potatoes, onions, carrots, apple and lemons with the olive oil, rosemary and sage and a good couple of grinds of salt and pepper.

Place them all in a large roasting tray with deep sides.

Place the turkey breasts among the vegetables and drizzle the remaining oil and herbs from the vegetable bowl over the top of the turkey. Rub the zest over the turkey breasts.

Place the roasting tray in the oven and roast for 30 minutes.

Remove from the oven and scatter over the cranberries, then turn the vegetables over.

Return to the oven and reduce the temperature to 190°C (375°F, Gas Mark 5).

Roast for another 50 minutes, until the turkey breasts are browned and cooked through.

Let the turkey rest for 10 minutes before serving.

Serve with the roast vegetables and apples and lemon quarters.

Chicken Burgers with Basil Pesto and Yoghurt Sauce

THIS HEALTHY BURGER OPTION BOASTS FANTASTIC FRESH FLAVOURS AND A CREAMY, ZESTY SAUCE

SERVES 8

BURGER PATTIES

1kg (2lb) chicken mince

2 large onions, grated and squeezed to remove excess liquid

2 large zucchinis, grated and squeezed to remove excess liquid

1 cup (125g, 4oz) breadcrumbs

¼ cup (30g, 1oz) Parmesan cheese, grated

1 egg, lightly beaten

2 tbsps olive oil

SAUCE

1½ cups (375g, 13oz) Greek yoghurt

¼ cup (50g, 2oz) cucumber, finely diced

2 cloves garlic, minced

1 tbsp fresh lemon juice

Salt, to taste

TO SERVE

8 bread rolls

½ cup (115g, 4oz) basil pesto

2 cups (100g, 3½ oz) micro greens

To make the patties, in a bowl, combine the chicken mince, onion, zucchini, breadcrumbs, Parmesan and egg.

Divide into 8 equal portions and form them into burger patties.

Place in the fridge for at least 1 hour.

To cook the patties, heat a grill pan or barbecue grill plate to high heat.

Brush the patties lightly with oil and grill for 5 minutes on either side, or until browned on the outside and cooked all the way through.

To make the sauce, mix all the ingredients together in a medium bowl until thoroughly combined.

To assemble, lightly toast the rolls, then layer over the bottom half of each a tablespoon of pesto, the patty, the yoghurt sauce, a layer of micro greens and then the top half of the roll.

Fish Fingers

SERVES 4

4 white fish fillets

1 egg

3 tbsps plain flour

¾ cup (90g, 3oz) Parmesan cheese, finely grated

¾ cup (90g, 3oz) panko (or use standard breadcrumbs)

Salt and pepper, to season

1 lemon, cut into wedges

2 cups (60g, 2oz) rocket leaves

Preheat oven to 220°C (425°F, Gas Mark 7) and butter a shallow baking dish. Set aside.

Debone the fish and cut into fingers. Pat fish fillets dry and season with salt and pepper.

Place the egg, flour, cheese and breadcrumbs in 4 separate bowls. Dip the fish pieces in each bowl starting with the egg and finishing with the breadcrumbs.

Put fish into the baking dish and transfer to the oven. Bake for 10 minutes, until fish is cooked and flakes easily with a fork. Remove from oven, serve on rocket leaves, with a wedge of lemon.

Garlic Aioli

MAKES ½ CUP

1 large egg yolk

2 tsps fresh lemon juice

Pinch of chilli powder

½ tsp American mustard

½ cup (125ml, 4fl oz) extra virgin olive oil

2 cloves garlic, minced

Salt and pepper, to taste

In a medium bowl, whisk together the egg yolk, lemon juice, chilli powder and mustard.

Add a few drops of oil at time to the egg mix and whisk it in vigorously each time.

The mixture should keep thickening into a smooth mayonnaise the more oil you add.

If it looks like it might be separating, keep whisking without adding any more oil until it goes back to a mayonnaise-like texture.

Keep adding the oil until it's finished.

Mix through the garlic and season to taste with salt and pepper.

CHIVES

These slender green herbs have a wondrous, sharp flavour that tastes like a mild onion combined with pungent lettuce. Chopped into small, perfect little circles, just a small sprinkle can bring cosy soups to life, adding a grassy crunch and a savoury bite. Pumpkin, potato and sweet potato soups are made for chive garnishes. Chives can also be the oomph in a very light dip — say cottage cheese or yoghurt and paprika. And shaken into a healthy lemon dressing, they make a simple salad of lettuce and cucumber feel luxurious.

Turkey and Ham Loaf

SERVES 8

1 tbsp olive oil, plus extra to brush

2 leeks, white part only, chopped

2 tbsp cognac (optional)

800g (1¾ lb) cooked turkey breasts cut into 1cm (½ in) chunks

500g (1lb) cooked ham, cut into 1cm (½ in) chunks

2 zucchinis, grated and squeezed to remove excess liquid

¼ cup (15g, ½ oz) semi-dried tomatoes, finely chopped

½ tsp freshly grated nutmeg

2 eggs, lightly beaten

1 tsp salt

½ tsp freshly ground pepper

Dill, to garnish

Preheat oven to 180°C (350°F, Gas Mark 5).

Line a 22 x 13cm (10 x 5in) loaf tin with baking paper.

Heat the oil in a large frying pan over medium-high heat. Add the leek and saute for 5 minutes, until it becomes softened and translucent. Add the cognac and let it simmer for 1 minute. Remove the mixture from the pan into a large mixing bowl and let it cool.

Once the leek has cooled, add the chopped turkey, ham, zucchini, tomatoes, nutmeg, eggs, salt and pepper. Mix together thoroughly.

Place the mixture into the lined loaf tin. Place the tin in a large roasting dish and fill the dish with enough water to come halfway up the sides of the loaf tin.

Bake in the oven for 1 hour and 20 minutes, or until a skewer inserted into the middle comes out clean.

Let sit for 10 minutes before serving.

Serve garnished with fresh dill sprigs.

Quinoa Pizza with Sun-Dried Tomatoes and Goat's Cheese

A PIZZA WITH A HEALTHY TWIST. THIS ONE MIGHT DISAPPEAR BEFORE YOUR VERY EYES SO WHY NOT MAKE A COUPLE

SERVES 2

CRUST

1 x 400g (14oz) can kidney beans, rinsed and drained

2 tbsps white chia seeds

2 tbsps ground flaxseeds

1 tsp sea salt

1 cup (170g, 6oz) quinoa, soaked in boiling water for 30 minutes

1 cup (125g, 4oz) sunflower seeds

Pinch of cayenne pepper

¼ cup (60ml, 2fl oz) olive oil

2 cloves garlic

TOPPINGS

½ cup (115g, 4oz) passata sauce

1 tsp mixed dried herbs

1 tbsp water

Pinch of salt and pepper

2 tomatoes, sliced

¼ cup (15g, ½ oz) semi-dried tomatoes, chopped

100g (3½ oz) goat's cheese

Handful of rocket leaves

Preheat oven to 180°C (350°F, Gas Mark 5). Lightly oil a large flat pizza tray.

Place all the ingredients for the crust in the bowl of a food processor and process until well combined but still with some texture.

Scrape the mixture out onto the pizza tray.

Press the mixture down and work it into a large flat circle, about 5mm (¼ in) thick. Roughly score with a sharp knife into slices. Bake in the oven for 20 minutes, or until dry and crisp to the touch.

Mix the passata sauce, dried herbs and water and spread over the base.

Top with the tomato slices, semi-dried tomatoes and dollops of goat's cheese. Sprinkle over some good grinds of salt and pepper.

Bake in the oven for 10 minutes to heat through. Remove and sprinkle over the rocket leaves.

Serve warm.

Spaghetti with Roasted Pumpkin, Bacon and Sage

SWEET PUMPKIN, SALTY BACON AND THE EARTHY TONES OF SAGE AND PINE NUTS COMBINE TO MAKE THIS SIMPLE DINNER A LOVELY ONE

SERVES 4

2 tbsps olive oil

3 cups (405g, 14oz) butternut pumpkin, cut into 1cm (½ in) cubes

1 tsp salt

¼ tsp freshly ground black pepper

400g (14oz) spaghetti

¼ cup (30g, 1oz) Parmesan cheese, grated

6 slices pancetta, cut into 3cm (1in) strips

¼ cup (10g, ¼ oz) fresh sage leaves, roughly chopped

2 tbsps pine nuts

Preheat oven to 220°C (425°F, Gas Mark 7). Line a large flat baking tray with baking paper.

Toss 1 tablespoon olive oil with the pumpkin cubes, salt and pepper. Place the cubes in an even layer on the baking tray. Bake for 30 minutes, or until tender.

Cook the spaghetti in a large pot of salted boiling water for 10 minutes, or until al dente. Before draining the pasta, reserve 1 cup of the pasta water.

Drain the pasta, return the spaghetti to the pot and stir through 1 tablespoon of the olive oil and the Parmesan. Set aside.

Heat a small frying pan over medium-high heat and fry the pancetta and half the sage leaves for 4 minutes, until crisp. Add the pine nuts and cook for 1 minute.

Add the pancetta mix and the pumpkin to the pot with the spaghetti.

Place the pot on medium heat and gently stir through the ingredients for 2 minutes until warmed through.

Serve garnished with the leftover sage leaves.

BUCKWHEAT PASTA

The sneaky truth about buckwheat is that it contains no wheat — buckwheat is a fruit seed and it is gluten-free and full of protein.

Buckwheat flour creates nutty, grainy noodles called soba noodles, which are beloved in Japanese cuisine. In Japan, soba noodles are classically served as a side to many meals, freshly cooked and chilled. They are eaten with a simple, savoury-sweet dipping sauce mixing rice wine, ginger and fish stock, topped with fresh spring onions. In Japan, there is a word for the soothing effect of soba noodles: 'nodogoshi', which means 'good throat-feel'.

Buckwheat also makes a delicious, earthy pasta, which can be store-bought or made at home, combining buckwheat flour, semolina or white flour, eggs, salt and water. To DIY, knead the mixture into dough, refrigerate for an hour, then roll it through a pasta machine to make flat, wide noodles like fettucine.

Without a pasta machine, more kneading and a rolling pin will do the job. Or it is simpler to pick the noodles up from the health-food store and start indulging in healthy, low-carb pasta dishes. As the noodles are comforting the belly, they're also lowering cholesterol and reducing and stabilizing blood sugar levels, which is helpful in the prevention of diabetes and obesity.

BUCKWHEAT COMFORT MEALS

BUCKWHEAT NOODLES WITH CARAMELISED ONIONS AND SAGE: Brown onions and sage with olive oil and butter and pour them over al dente noodles. The onions will be juicy and sweet and blend with the fragrance of sage, a pungent green herb that becomes lemony in this warm dish.

CREAMY BUCKWHEAT PASTA WITH MUSHROOMS: Toss a medley of mushrooms — shitake, cremini and oyster — into olive oil, butter, pepper and a splash of cream. Garnish with crumbled Parmesan cheese and fresh, chopped parsley.

BUCKWHEAT MAC AND CHEESE: Saute chopped silverbeet with garlic and stir through noodles. Pour in egg and grated Parmesan, then bake the noodles for a warm, gooey dish. Potato chunks will fill this out and Cheddar cheese will give extra melty cream.

SOBA NOODLES WITH KIMCHI AND EGGS: Kimchi, a traditional side dish in Korea, is fermented cabbage marinated in garlic and red chillies. Make it at home or buy in a jar from Asian supermarkets. Toss kimchi through the cooked soba noodles. Add medium-boiled eggs, chopped in half. Season with spring onions and sesame seeds. This is a hybrid comfort dish, part Korean, Japanese and Western.

Black Sesame Udon Noodles

SERVES 4

450g (1lb) udon noodles

3 tbsps sesame oil

1 clove garlic, minced

1 tbsp fresh ginger, minced

1 tsp chilli powder

¼ cup (40g, 1½ oz) black sesame seeds

¼ cup (60ml, 2fl oz) tamari

6 tbsps mirin

2 tsps rice wine vinegar

1 tsp maple syrup

¼ cup (10g, ¼ oz) fresh mint leaves, shredded

Boil the noodles in boiling water and cook according to the package instructions. Drain and mix with 1 teaspoon sesame oil.

Heat the rest of oil in a small frying pan over medium heat. Add the garlic, ginger and chilli powder and fry for 1 minute. Add the sesame seeds, tamari, mirin, vinegar and maple syrup and heat for 4 minutes.

Stir the sauce through the noodles. Serve the noodles warm, with the mint leaves mixed through.

Buckwheat Noodle Salad

SERVES 4

¼ cup (40g, 1½ oz) white and black sesame seeds

230g (8oz) buckwheat soba noodles

2 tbsps sesame oil

3 carrots, finely julienned

1 cup (175g, 6oz) soybeans

1 bunch asparagus, ends trimmed, sliced into thin strips

4 tbsps lemon juice

6 tbsps tamari

2 cloves garlic, crushed

2 tbsps fresh ginger, minced

1½ tsps maple syrup

5 spring onions, thinly sliced on the diagonal

Dry-fry sesame seeds for 2 minutes. Remove from heat and set aside. Cook noodles until al dente according to packet directions. Drain, rinse under cold water, stir through 1 teaspoon sesame oil and set aside. Heat 1 teaspoon sesame oil in a wok over high heat. Add carrot, soybeans, spring onion and asparagus and stir-fry for 3 minutes then add them to the noodles. Whisk together the lemon juice, tamari, garlic, ginger, maple syrup and rest of the oil. Pour over the noodles and vegetables and gently toss to combine. Serve immediately with the sesame seeds sprinkled over as garnish.

BLACK SESAME SEEDS

These nutrient-rich seeds are a nutty and good-looking addition to a stir-fry or smoothie. The Chinese believe these humble little seeds can correct an energy imbalance in the body, reversing the bodily signs of anxiety and ageing (that would be wrinkles, grey hair and memory loss) — so there's that benefit, too.

MISO

Miso is a paste made from fermented soybeans. Its intense flavour features in the majority of Japanese dishes. It tastes like soy sauce that has been whipped into a moist puree.

Home-made or store-bought miso paste can be kept in the fridge for months and used in a variety of different ways, including as the base for dressings, sauces and marinades, and as the first step to every Japanese meal: miso soup.

Miso soup is cosy and tasty and can both energize and soothe after a long day. Add hot water and it's salty and a little cloudy. It usually has cubes of tofu and spring onion floating around in it. It can be an appetizer, or it can be a whole dish filled out with buckwheat or rice noodles and any sort of vegetable.

To make miso soup at home is quite easy. Mix 1 tablespoon of white miso paste with 1 cup of plain water. Add dashi stock, which is the fishy stock used in most Japanese noodle soups and sold in Asian groceries or stocked in the Asian food aisle. Throw in a few sheets of nori seaweed — the dark green, crunchy, grainy sheets that are also used to roll around fish to make sushi rolls.

WHITE MISO (SHIRO MISO)

White miso is fermented for just a few days and the result is a sweetness that is a little vinegary when mixed with bright herbs like coriander, spring onion or parsley. White miso is perfect for home-made miso soup. It is lower in salt than darker varieties and has a mellower, more delicate flavour. It's also perfect for salad dressings and noodle sauces — mix a small spoonful with ginger, rice bran oil, sesame oil and lime juice and throw it over a bowl of buckwheat noodles. And for the ultimate comfort food, melt white miso paste over a tray of warm, roasted or mashed potatoes.

YELLOW MISO (SHINSHU MISO)

This is a little more fragrant and salty than white miso and comes with a golden tinge. Yellow miso is excellent for glazing fish — a fillet of salmon is a whole new creature when baked with yellow miso.

RED MISO (AKA MISO)

Red miso is excellent for marinating meat. It is salty and a bit smoky and pops when seasoned with spring onions, lime or lemongrass. A little bit of brown sugar can mellow it out. Add a Japanese twist to a roast leg of lamb or pork, or mix it in with chunks of tuna and avocado for a creamy, powerful salad, tossed with sesame seeds.

Chicken Ramen

THIS REHYDRATING JAPANESE BROTH IS GOOD FOR BOTH BODY AND SOUL

SERVES 2

2 chicken breasts

Salt and pepper, to season

1 tbsp butter

2 tsps sesame or vegetable oil

3 tsps fresh garlic, minced

2 tsps fresh ginger, minced

3 tbsps soy sauce

2 tbsps mirin

4 cups (1L, 2pt) rich chicken stock

½ tsp chilli powder

25g (1oz) dried shitake mushrooms (optional)

1 bunch baby bok choy, cut into 2cm (1in) slices

1 tsp salt

2 eggs

180g (6oz) ramen noodles (dried or fresh)

¼ cup (50g, 2oz) spring onions, sliced

1 bird's-eye chilli, sliced

1 tbsp sesame seeds

Preheat the oven to 190°C (375°F, Gas Mark 5). Season the chicken generously with salt and pepper. Melt the butter in a large oven-safe frying pan. Add the chicken, skin side down, and fry for 5–6 minutes or until golden brown. Flip and fry a further 4–5 minutes, until golden. Transfer the pan to the oven and roast for 15–20 minutes, until the chicken is cooked through. Remove from the oven, transfer the chicken to a plate and cover with foil until ready to serve.

Heat the oil in a large pot over medium heat, until shimmering. Add the garlic and ginger, and cook until softened. Add the soy sauce and mirin, and stir to combine. Cook for another 1 minute. Add the stock and chilli powder, cover, and bring to boil. Remove the lid and let simmer uncovered for 5 minutes, then add the mushrooms and bok choy. Simmer gently for another 10 minutes, and season with salt, to taste. Remove the bok choy from the mix and set aside.

Fill a pot with sufficient water to cover the eggs, and bring to a boil. Gently lower the eggs into the boiling water, and simmer for 7 minutes. Retain the boiling water. Remove eggs and rinse in cold water. When cool enough to handle, peel away the shells and slice in half.

Add the ramen noodles to the boiling water. Cook for 2–3 minutes, until soft, then divide the noodles into two large bowls. Slice the chicken and add to the bowl. Garnish with spring onions, soft boiled egg, bok choy, chilli slices and sesame seeds. Serve immediately.

Seared Salmon in Ginger Broth

A LOVELY, SIMPLE BROTH WITH GINGER DOING ITS CALMING, ANTI-INFLAMMATORY THING, WHILE FISH GIVES YOU A PROTEIN BOOST

SERVES 2

4 cups (1L, 2pt) vegetable stock

1 tbsp miso paste

2 tbsps sesame oil

1 tbsp fresh ginger, minced

180g (6oz) soba noodles

2 spring onions, green part only, sliced

320g (11oz) salmon fillet cut into 2 equal pieces, no skin, bones removed

Salt and freshly ground pepper

Heat the stock in a large saucepan and bring to the boil. Reduce the heat to low, stir in the miso paste, 1 teaspoon sesame oil and ginger and simmer for 5 minutes. Turn off the heat, cover and let it sit for 15 minutes.

Bring back to the boil and add the spring onion and noodles. Reduce heat and simmer the noodles for 4 minutes. Turn off the heat and let it sit while you cook the salmon.

Brush the salmon with the rest of the sesame oil.

Heat a small frying pan over medium-high heat. Place the salmon in the pan and cook for 4 minutes. Carefully flip the fillets over and fry for another 4 minutes. Let the salmon sit for 2 minutes.

To serve, divide the soba noodles among 2 soup bowls. Spoon out the broth into each bowl and place a piece of salmon on each.

Garnish with the spring onions from the broth.

Fennel and Parsley Vegetable Broth

THIS BEAUTIFUL CLEAR BROTH CAN BE EATEN AS
IT IS OR USED AS A BASE FOR OTHER DISHES

MAKES 2.5 LITRES

1 tbsp olive oil

2 large leeks, white part only, chopped

1 onion, roughly chopped

8 stalks celery, chopped

2 large carrots, roughly chopped

1 small fennel bulb, chopped

1 head of garlic, halved crosswise

1/3 cup (80ml, 3fl oz) dry white wine

1 tsp black peppercorns

2 bay leaves

5 stalks each of thyme and flat-leaf parsley

Salt and pepper to taste

Heat oil in a large stockpot over medium-high heat.

Add the leek, onion, celery, carrot and fennel and cook for 6 minutes.

Add the remaining ingredients and 3.5 litres (7pt 6fl oz) of water.

Bring to a boil, then reduce heat to a simmer.

Cover and let simmer for at least 2 hours.

Season to taste.

Serve hot with the vegetables or strained as a consommé.

This broth can be made 3 days ahead.

Mushroom, Chicken and Spinach Soup

THIS LIGHT AND DELICATE SOUP IS PACKED WITH FRESH VEGETABLES THAT PACK A HEALTHY PUNCH

SERVES 6

2 tbsps olive oil

1 onion, chopped

2 cloves garlic, minced

400g (14oz) button mushrooms, sliced

3 stalks celery, chopped

600g (1lb 5oz) chicken breasts, sliced

1½ cups (75g, 3oz) baby spinach leaves

2 bird's-eye chillies, seeded and sliced

Salt and pepper, to taste

STOCK

1 chicken carcass

1 large onion, chopped

2 carrots, chopped

3 stalks celery, chopped

1 tsp black peppercorns

2 stalks flat-leaf parlsey

2 bay leaves

Salt and pepper

To make the stock, place all the stock ingredients into a large stock pot along with 3 litres (6pt 5fl oz) of water.

Bring to a boil. Reduce the heat and simmer, covered, for 3 hours. Use a large flat spoon to skim off any froth that is floating on the top while it's cooking.

Leave to cool, then strain through a fine mesh sieve.

To make the soup, heat the oil in a large saucepan over medium-high heat. Add the onion and garlic and saute for 5 minutes, until the onion is translucent.

Add the sliced mushrooms and celery and fry for a further 5 minutes.

Add the chicken and fry for another 5 minutes.

Pour 2 litres (4pt 4fl oz) of the stock into the pot and bring to a boil.

Reduce the heat to low and add the spinach leaves and chilli and simmer for 2 minutes, until the spinach leaves are just wilted.

Serve immediately with a sprinkling of salt and pepper.

Roasted Pumpkin Soup with Spicy Baked Chickpeas

VELVETY SMOOTH SOUP AND CRUNCHY CHICKPEAS CREATE A SPECIAL AND COMFORTING DISH THAT'S PERFECT FOR A WINTER'S EVENING

SERVES 4

SOUP

1 whole butternut pumpkin, peeled, deseeded and cut into 3cm (1in) chunks

1 onion, peeled and halved

3 tbsps olive oil

Salt and pepper, to season

4 cups (1L, 2pt) vegetable stock

½ cup (125ml, 4fl oz) cream

CHICKPEAS

1 x 400g (14oz) can chickpeas, thoroughly drained and rinsed

1 tbsp olive oil

½ tsp ground cumin

½ tsp chilli powder

¼ tsp cayenne pepper

½ tsp sea salt

Preheat the oven to 200°C (400°F, Gas Mark 6) and line two baking trays with baking paper.

Place the pumpkin and onion on the baking tray. Drizzle with olive oil and season with salt and pepper. Toss to coat the vegetables with the seasoned oil.

Place the chickpeas in a large bowl and toss with the olive oil, cumin, chilli, cayenne and sea salt until evenly coated. Spread the chickpeas in an even layer on the second baking tray.

Place both trays in the oven and roast for 40 minutes or until the pumpkin is soft and golden and chickpeas crisp and golden. Remove from oven. Place the pumpkin and onion and half of the chickpeas in a saucepan and allow to cool slightly. Set aside the remaining chickpeas to use as a garnish later.

Add a quarter of the vegetable stock to the saucepan and blend all the ingredients in the saucepan with a stick blender (or transfer to a stand blender).

Gradually add the rest of the stock, blending a few times in between each addition.

Add the cream and stir through gently.

Bring the soup to a low simmer and cook for 5 minutes, until heated through. Serve with fresh pepper and reserved chickpeas.

Vegan Chocolate Nut Truffles

MAKES 18

1 cup (125g, 4oz) raw macadamia nuts

Water, as needed

½ cup (180g, 6oz) maple syrup

½ cup (60g, 2oz) cacao powder

½ cup (60g, 2oz) dates, pitted

½ cup (60g, 2oz) chopped nuts, for rolling

2 tbsps cacao powder

Place the macadamias in a food processor or high-speed blender and process until finely ground. Slowly add a little water and process again until a thick paste forms. Add dates and continue to process until incorporated. Add maple syrup and cacao powder and briefly process until combined. Using damp hands roll the mixture into balls of the desired size.

Prepare a baking tray by lining with baking paper.

To prepare for rolling the truffles, clean and dry a work surface and sprinkle cacao powder and chopped nuts in two separate areas. Roll the truffles in the desired coating and then place on the prepared tray.

Transfer to the fridge to chill for a minimum of 3 hours.

Mango & Orange Pudding

SERVES 8

1½ cups (240g, 8oz) pureed fresh mango

½ cup (125ml, 4fl oz) fresh strained orange juice

½ cup (125ml, 4fl oz) coconut cream (use the thick cream from the top of the unshaken can)

½ cup (125ml, 4fl oz) water

⅓ cup (70g, 2½ oz) sugar

1 tbsp plus ½ tsp unflavoured gelatin

Place the gelatin, sugar and water in a small saucepan and bring to the boil.

Reduce the heat to low, stir in the mango puree, orange juice and coconut cream, remove from heat.

Lightly oil the moulds with canola or vegetable oil.

Pour in the mango mixture into 8 small moulds.

Chill till set for at least 3 hours.

Carefully turn out the puddings from the moulds onto small serving plates.

DARK CHOCOLATE

Don't consider giving up chocolate for another second. Dark chocolate is rich and luxurious, and it's been given the thumbs up by nutritionists. Just a square of it can satisfy a sweet craving and it will give an energy boost like caffeine with only positive side effects. A bowl of dark chocolate mousse made with coconut milk and maple syrup (rather than heavy cream and sugar) could actually be considered a health food even if it's consumed while lying on the couch.

Chocolate Loaf Cake with Berries and Coconut Cream Sauce

BEETROOT AND BERRIES GIVE THIS CAKE IT'S RICH RED COLOUR —
AND PROVIDE ANTIOXIDANTS, VITAMINS AND MINERALS TOO

SERVES 10

CAKE

100g (3½ oz) dark chocolate

250g (9oz) beetroot, peeled and cooked

⅔ cup (150ml, 5fl oz) vegetable oil

3 eggs, room temperature

¾ cup (260g, 9oz) maple syrup

1 tsp vanilla extract

250g (9oz) plain flour

2 tsp baking powder

1 tbsp cacao powder

¾ cup (100g, 3½ oz) raspberries

COCONUT CREAM SAUCE

1 cup (175g, 6oz) white chocolate chips

2 tbsps coconut cream

TO SERVE

1 cup (100g, 3½ oz) blueberries

1 cup (125g, 4oz) blackberries

Sprigs of fresh thyme

Preheat oven to 180°C (350°F, Gas Mark 5). Line a 22 x 13cm (10 x 5in) loaf tin with baking paper.

Gently melt the chocolate in a bowl placed over a saucepan filled with 3cm (1in) of simmering water.

Puree the beetroot in a food processor until smooth. Pour in the oil and mix through. Add the eggs one at a time, ensuring they're completely blended in before adding the next one. Then mix through the maple syrup and vanilla extract.

Mix the flour, baking powder and cacao powder and make a well in the centre. Add the mixture from the processor and stir thoroughly.

Stir in the chocolate and raspberries. Pour into the loaf tin and bake for 50 minutes, or until a skewer inserted into the middle comes out clean.

Cool in the tin, then lift out onto a wire rack to cool.

To make the white chocolate frosting, stir together the white chocolate chips and coconut cream in a large bowl. Place over a saucepan with 3cm of simmering water. Gently stir until the chocolate is melted. Remove and pour over cake.

Serve the cake warm with the blueberries and blackberries and a sprig or two of thyme to garnish.

Vegan Chocolate Chia Pudding

THIS DESSERT IS SIMPLE, DELICIOUS AND HEALTHY: ALL YOUR HAPPINESS BOXES TICKED!

SERVES 2

2½ tbsps chia seeds

2½ tbsps raw cacao powder (or cocoa powder)

6 medjool dates, pitted

1 cup (250ml, 8fl oz) almond milk

TO SERVE

1 banana, sliced

2 tbsps goji berries, chopped

1 purple fig, quartered

20g (¾ oz) chocolate, shaved

Place chia seeds, cacao powder and dates in a large bowl. Pour over the almond milk and set aside for 30 minutes. (If you have a high-speed blender, you can skip this step.)

Place in a blender and blitz for 2–3 minutes until smooth. Taste and add more cacao, for chocolatey flavour, or dates, for sweetness, to suit your tastes.

Garnish with banana, goji berries, fig and shaved (vegan) chocolate as desired.

Blueberry Ice Cream Mess with Lavender Flowers

THIS GORGEOUS DESSERT JUST SHOWS: THE HEALTHIEST LIFE CAN BE THE TASTIEST ONE TOO!

SERVES 8

3 cups (750ml, 1pt 9fl oz) coconut cream

1 cup (250ml, 8fl oz) soy milk

1 tsp vanilla extract

8 egg yolks

1 cup (220g, 8oz) caster sugar (use sugar substitute such as stevia if desired)

1 cup (100g, 3½ oz) fresh blueberries

¼ cup (90g, 3oz) maple syrup

8 stalks lavender flowers

Combine the cream, milk and vanilla in a large saucepan over medium heat. Bring to a simmer, then remove from the heat and let cool for at least 30 minutes.

Beat the egg yolks and sugar until thick and pale.

Add the cream mixture in small batches, until thoroughly combined.

Pour the mix into a saucepan and heat over low heat for 20 minutes, stirring constantly.

The mixture will thicken into a custard. Let it sit for 10 minutes.

Pour into an airtight container and place in the fridge for 3 hours.

Meanwhile, combine the blueberries and maple syrup in a medium saucepan over medium heat. Stir for 5 minutes, until the blueberries are starting to release their juices. Turn off the heat and let cool to room temperature.

Place the ice cream and blueberries in an ice-cream machine and churn for 30 minutes, until thickened enough to go into the freezer.

Remove from the machine and place in an airtight ice-cream container.

Freeze for at least 4 hours, preferably overnight.

Remove an hour before serving and allow to thaw. Just before serving, place in the blender and process until just soft. Spoon into serving bowls and serve garnished with lavender flowers.

Index

almonds
  almond chocolate milk 66
  raw chocolate mousse cake with dark
    chocolate sauce 74
  spaghetti with pesto and toasted almonds
    flakes 88
anchovies 27
apple
  baked apples with honey and walnuts 124
  raisin compote 118
  slow-cooked pork with apple sauce 166
avocado
  avocado fries with yoghurt dip 25
  green salad 186
  hipster salad with avocado vinaigrette 22
  kale salad 25
  Paleo chocolate mousse 72
bacon
  liver baked with mushrooms and bacon 184
  spaghetti with roasted pumpkin, bacon
    and sage 270
barley
  broad bean and barley salad 34
  home-made blood sausage 188
basil
  spaghetti with pesto and toasted almond
    flakes 88
beans 241
  broad bean and barley salad 34
  broad bean hummus 246
  edamame 35
  edamame and parsley salad 34
  warm roasted vegetable salad with herb
    dressing 248
beef
  beef and golden beetroot stew 162
  beef sirloin with horseradish cream 44
beetroot 145
  beef and golden beetroot stew 162
  chocolate loaf cake with berries and
    coconut cream sauce 294
berries 119, *see also* **blueberries, raspberries, strawberries**
  berry and yoghurt popsicles 132
  chocolate loaf cake with berries and
    coconut cream sauce 294
  raw coconut and berry cheesecakes 76
black sesame seeds 275
blood 177
  home-made blood sausage 188
blueberries
  blueberry ice cream mess with lavender
    flowers 298
  blueberry quinoa muffins 118
  dairy-free blueberry and cacao ice cream 70
bok choy 87
  chicken ramen 280
  red curry salmon with sauteed greens 20
  roasted baby bok choy 95
broccoli 87
Brussels sprouts
  pickled sprouts 199
  warm roasted vegetable salad 248
buckwheat
  buckwheat pasta 273
cabbage
  red and green cabbage sauerkraut 196

cacao
  chocolate berry balls 120
  dairy-free blueberry and cacao
    ice cream 70
  Paleo chocolate mousse 72
  raw chocolate mousse cake with dark
    chocolate sauce 74
  vegan chocolate chia pudding 296
  vegan chocolate nut truffles 292
calamari
  spicy calamari in tomato sauce 38
capsicum
  roasted capsicum soup 210
  roasted stuffed capsicums 212
cashews
  raw chocolate mousse cake with dark
    chocolate sauce 74
  raw coconut and berry cheesecakes 76
  raw coconut slice with raspberries 116
cauliflower
  roasted cauliflower tacos with chipotle-
    tahini sauce 216
  roasted cauliflower with lemon and tahini
    sauce 182
  cauliflower mash with tofu 236
cheese
  quinoa pizza with sun-dried tomatoes and
    goat's cheese 268
chia
  chia pot with baked figs and honey 114
  vegan chocolate chia pudding 296
chicken
  chicken burgers with basil pesto and
    yoghurt sauce 262
  chicken ramen 280
  coconut chicken noodle bowl 40
  green chicken curry 100
  mushroom, chicken and spinach soup 286
  roasted chicken with lemon, garlic and
    olives 170
  steamed ginger chicken 42
chickpeas
  chickpea and zucchini rissole with
    sprouted greens 258
  pumpkin and chickpea burger with the
    lot 250
  roasted pumpkin soup with spicy baked
    chickpeas 288
Chinese broccoli
  pork belly with shoestring onions and
    Chinese broccoli 172
  red curry salmon with sauteed greens 20
chives 265
chocolate. *see also* **cacao**
  almond chocolate milk 66
  chocolate loaf cake with berries and
    coconut cream sauce 294
coconut
  chocolate berry balls 120
  chocolate loaf cake with berries and
    coconut cream sauce 294
  lemon coconut bars 78
  raw coconut slice with raspberries 116
coconut milk 99
  coconut chicken noodle bowl 40
  coconut ice cream 104
  coconut lentil curry 242

cranberries
  kale and quinoa salad with cranberries 90
  roast turkey breast with potatoes and
    cranberries 260
cucumber
  green salad 186
duck
  pan-seared duck breast 46
eggplant 223
  eggplant chips and tomato sauce 226
  eggplant pate 226
  eggplant tofu teriyaki 232
  roasted eggplant, spinach and quinoa
    salad with miso dressing 228
  roasted stuffed capsicums 212
  stuffed eggplants with pistachios 224
fennel
  fennel and parsley vegetable broth 284
fig
  chia pot with baked figs and honey 114
fish 27, *see also* **salmon**
  fish fingers with sauce 264
  fresh fish tacos with yoghurt dressing 28
  Mediterranean baked trout 32
  moqueca de peixe (Brazilian fish stew) 102
  risotto with smoked fish 30
flaxseed 51
  flaxseed dukkah 50
  flaxseed salad and miso dressing 50
garlic
  garlic aioli 264
garlic chive flowers 237
ginger
  ginger biscuits 84
  ginger lemon kombucha tea 194
  seared salmon in ginger broth 282
  steamed ginger chicken 42
grapefruit
  pink grapefruit sorbet 134
ham
  turkey and ham loaf 266
hazelnuts 73
honey
  baked apples with honey and walnuts 124
  chia pot with baked figs and honey 114
  citrus and honey ice cream 130
  raw honey 129
honeydew
  detox green smoothie 72
horseradish
  beef sirloin with horseradish cream 44
kale 87
  kale and quinoa salad 56
  kale and quinoa salad with cranberries 90
  kale salad 25
kiwi fruit
  detox green smoothie 72
lamb
  lamb broth with grilled chops 164
lemon
  ginger lemon kombucha tea 194
  lemon coconut bars 78
  roasted cauliflower with lemon and tahini
    sauce 182
  roasted chicken with lemon, garlic and
    olives 170

lentils 241
coconut lentil curry 242
red lentil soup 244
stuffed sweet potato 236
liver 177
chicken liver pate 180
fried liver with onions 178
liver baked with mushrooms and
bacon 184
macadamias
macadamia nut cheese 68
vegan chocolate nut truffles 292
mango
crispy baked tofu with wild rice and
mango 234
mango and orange pudding 292
miso 279
flaxseed salad and miso dressing 50
roasted eggplant, spinach and quinoa
salad with miso dressing 228
mushroom
liver with mushrooms and bacon 184
mushroom, chicken and spinach soup 286
pickled mushrooms 174
sauteed mushrooms 174
shitake mushrooms 175
mussels
moqueca de peixe (Brazilian fish stew) 102
mustard greens 87
noodles
black sesame udon noodles 274
buckwheat noodle salad 274
chicken ramen 280
coconut chicken noodle bowl 40
nuts 241, *see also* **almonds, hazelnuts,**
macadamias, pecans, pistachios,
walnuts
nut milk 65
vegan chocolate nut truffles 292
oats
pumpkin oat scones 146
offal 177
okra 94
okra with tomatoes 95
prawn and okra ratatouille 92
olive oil 227
olives
roasted chicken with lemon, garlic and
olives 170
onion 145
caramelised red onion tartlets 148
fried liver with onions 178
pork belly with shoestring onions and
Chinese broccoli 172
orange
citrus and honey ice cream 130
mango and orange pudding 292
oysters 27
pasta
buckwheat pasta 273
spaghetti with pesto and toasted almond
flakes 88
spaghetti with roasted pumpkin, bacon
and sage 270
pastry
caramelised red onion tartlets 148
strawberry galette 122

peanut butter
peanut butter smoothie 82
peanuts 83
creamy peanut butter 82
pear
kale salad 25
peas 241
pecans
Paleo vegan cookies 200
pistachios
stuffed eggplants with pistachio
crumble 224
polenta
strawberry and redcurrant polenta
cake 142
pomegranate
hipster salad with avocado vinaigrette 22
pork
home-made blood sausage 188
pork belly with shoestring onions and
Chinese broccoli 172
quick quinoa and pork meatballs 54
slow-cooked pork with apple sauce 166
potato
roast turkey breast with potatoes and
cranberries 260
warm potato salad 246
prawns
moqueca de peixe (Brazilian fish stew) 102
prawn and okra ratatouille 92
pumpkin
20-minute pumpkin butter 150
hipster salad with avocado vinaigrette 22
pumpkin and chickpea burger 250
pumpkin and spinach no-pasta
lasagne 214
pumpkin bread 150
pumpkin fruit cookies 152
pumpkin oat scones 146
roasted pumpkin soup with spicy baked
chickpeas 288
spaghetti with roasted pumpkin, bacon
and sage 270
warm roasted vegetable salad with herb
dressing 248
quinoa 53
blueberry quinoa muffins 118
hipster salad with avocado vinaigrette 22
kale and quinoa salad 56
kale salad with cranberries
and kale 90
quick quinoa and pork meatballs 54
quinoa pizza with sun-dried tomatoes
and goat's cheese 268
roasted eggplant, spinach and quinoa
salad with miso dressing 228
raisins
raisin compote 118
raspberries
chocolate berry balls 120
raw coconut slice with raspberries 116
redcurrants
strawberry and redcurrant polenta
cake 142
rhubarb 141
red cordial 140
rhubarb and white chocolate tart 138
rhubarb jam 140

rice
crispy baked tofu with wild rice and
mango 234
risotto with smoked fish 30
rocket 187
green salad 186
rosemary 198
salmon 27
red curry salmon with sauteed greens 20
seared salmon in ginger broth 282
teriyaki salmon bowl 18
silverbeet 87
spinach
detox green smoothie 72
mushroom, chicken and spinach soup 286
pumpkin and spinach no-pasta
lasagne 214
roasted eggplant, spinach and quinoa
salad with miso dressing 228
wilted baby spinach salad 186
strawberries
red cordial 140
strawberry and redcurrant polenta
cake 142
strawberry galette 122
sultanas
Paleo vegan cookies 200
sweet potato 145
stuffed sweet potato 236
tofu 231
crispy baked tofu with wild rice and
mango 234
eggplant tofu teriyaki 232
cauliflower mash with tofu 236
tomato
eggplant chips and tomato sauce 226
okra with tomatoes 95
quinoa pizza with sun-dried tomatoes
and goat's cheese 268
spicy calamari in tomato sauce 38
zucchini pasta with sun-dried tomato
sauce 218
tuna 27
turkey
roast turkey breast with potatoes and
cranberries 260
turkey and ham loaf 266
walnuts
baked apples with honey and
walnuts 124
spaghetti with pesto and toasted almond
flakes 88
white chocolate
rhubarb and white chocolate tart 138
yoghurt 193
avocado fries with yoghurt dip 25
berry and yoghurt popsicles 132
chicken burgers with basil pesto and
yoghurt sauce 262
fresh fish tacos with yoghurt dressing 28
zucchini 145
chickpea and zucchini rissole with
sprouted greens 258
pickled zucchini 199
zucchini pasta with sun-dried tomato
sauce 218

HERRON
book distributors PTY LTD

First Published in 2017 by Herron Book Distributors Pty Ltd
14 Manton St
Morningside
QLD 4170
www.herronbooks.com

WWW.CAPTAINHONEY.COM.AU

Custom book production by Captain Honey Pty Ltd
PO Box 155
Byron Bay
NSW 2481
www.captainhoney.com.au

Cataloguing-in-Publication. A catalogue record for this book is available from the National Library of Australia

ISBN 978-0-947163-59-4

Printed and bound in China by Shenzhen Jinhao Color Printing Co., Ltd

5 4 3 2 1   17 18 19 20 21

NOTES FOR THE READER

All reasonable efforts have been made to ensure the accuracy of the content in this book. Information in this book is not intended as a substitute for medical advice. The author and publisher cannot and do not accept any legal duty of care or responsibility in relation to the content in this book, and disclaim any liabilities relating to its use.

PHOTO CREDITS